Pro Java Clustering and Scalability

Building Real-Time Apps with Spring, Cassandra, Redis, WebSocket and RabbitMQ

Jorge Acetozi

Apress®

Pro Java Clustering and Scalability: Building Real-Time Apps with Spring, Cassandra, Redis, WebSocket and RabbitMQ

Jorge Acetozi
São Paulo / SP, Brazil

ISBN-13 (pbk): 978-1-4842-2984-2   ISBN-13 (electronic): 978-1-4842-2985-9
DOI 10.1007/978-1-4842-2985-9

Library of Congress Control Number: 2017951201

Cover image by Freepik (`www.freepik.com`)

Managing Director: Welmoed Spahr
Editorial Director: Todd Green
Acquisitions Editor: Steve Anglin
Development Editor: Matthew Moodie
Technical Reviewer: Massimo Nardone
Coordinating Editor: Mark Powers
Copy Editor: Kim Wimpsett

Distributed to the book trade worldwide by Springer Science+Business Media New York, 233 Spring Street, 6th Floor, New York, NY 10013. Phone 1-800-SPRINGER, fax (201) 348-4505, e-mail orders-ny@springer-sbm.com, or visit `www.springeronline.com`. Apress Media, LLC is a California LLC and the sole member (owner) is Springer Science + Business Media Finance Inc (SSBM Finance Inc). SSBM Finance Inc is a **Delaware** corporation.

For information on translations, please e-mail rights@apress.com, or visit `www.apress.com/rights-permissions`.

Apress titles may be purchased in bulk for academic, corporate, or promotional use. eBook versions and licenses are also available for most titles. For more information, reference our Print and eBook Bulk Sales web page at `www.apress.com/bulk-sales`.

Any source code or other supplementary material referenced by the author in this book is available to readers on GitHub via the book's product page, located at `www.apress.com/9781484229842`. For more detailed information, please visit `www.apress.com/source-code`.

Printed on acid-free paper

This book never would have been published without my wife Juliana's daily support and patience. Thank you so much. I love you!

Contents at a Glance

Contents

About the Author

Jorge Acetozi is a software engineer who spends almost his whole day having fun with things such as AWS, CoreOS, Kubernetes, Docker, Terraform, Ansible, Cassandra, Redis, Elasticsearch, Graylog, New Relic, Sensu, Elastic Stack, Fluentd, RabbitMQ, Kafka, Java, Spring, and much more! He loves deploying applications in production while thousands of users are online, monitoring the infrastructure, and acting quickly when monitoring tools decide to challenge his heart's health!

About the Technical Reviewer

Massimo Nardone has more than 23 years of experience in security, web/mobile development, cloud computing, and IT architecture. His true IT passions are security and Android.

He has been programming and teaching how to program with Android, Perl, PHP, Java, VB, Python, C/C++, and MySQL for more than 20 years.

He has a master of science degree in computing science from the University of Salerno in Italy.

He has worked as a project manager, software engineer, research engineer, chief security architect, information security manager, PCI/SCADA auditor, and senior lead IT security/cloud/SCADA architect.

In addition, he has been a visiting lecturer and supervisor for exercises at the Networking Laboratory of the Helsinki University of Technology (Aalto University), and he holds four international patents (PKI, SIP, SAML, and proxy areas).

He currently works as the chief information security officer (CISO) for Cargotec Oyj and is a member of the ISACA Finland Chapter board.

Massimo has reviewed more than 40 IT books for different publishing companies and is the coauthor of *Pro Android Games* (Apress, 2015).

Introduction

My name is Jorge Acetozi, and I'm a Brazilian software engineer who has worked for many years as a Java developer. During my career, I have been interested in subjects such as these:

- Linux

- Distributed systems

- Testing automation

- Continuous integration

- Continuous delivery

- Cloud computing

- Virtualization

- Containerization

- Security

Why the varied interests? I just didn't feel that coding in Java only was enough for me professionally (although doing this while following best practices is not an easy task). I wanted to understand the entire process of creating software and delivering it to a production environment.

So, some years ago I started a career as a DevOps engineer.

After taking these two paths, I've noticed there are two types of software engineer. In the first group are developers who usually don't feel excited by infrastructure subjects and merely want to write code following best practices. However, this means they are not able to maintain a production environment since it involves much more than just writing software code.

In the second group are infrastructure people who usually hate writing software code (note that writing small scripts to automate infrastructure tasks are quite different than writing software code). On the other hand, these people are able to maintain a production environment because they understand the deployment process, how to monitor the servers, how to handle security issues, and so on.

The software engineer I'm trying to become sits right in the middle of these types of developers and infrastructure folks. I'd like to be an excellent programmer who follows coding best practices, but I also want to be able to put code into production and maintain it.

Why I Wrote This Book

This is a programming book but with many interesting infrastructure discussions and tips. I have coded an entire chat application using the Spring Framework, WebSocket, Cassandra, Redis, RabbitMQ, and MySQL, and I discuss how you can horizontally scale this application implementing a WebSocket multinode architecture. In my opinion, this is what makes this book different from others.

My objective when writing this book was to bring you a new experience by mixing a lot of development code with interesting and didactic infrastructure discussions. I'm sure you'll really enjoy it!

To keep in touch with me, please follow me on the following:

- My web site[1]
- GitHub[2]
- Twitter[3]
- Facebook[4]

Who This Book Is For

This book is suitable for every software developer with at least a few years of experience. In other words, this is not a book to learn the basics of Spring, JUnit, and Mockito, for example.

All the code in the chat application is explained in detail, except the very basics. Just to give an idea of what I'm talking about, take a look at this example:

```
@Configuration
@EnableScheduling
@EnableWebSocketMessageBroker
public class WebSocketConfigSpringSession extends AbstractSessionWeb
SocketMessageBrokerConfigurer<ExpiringSession>  {
  @Value("${ebook.chat.relay.host}")
  private String relayHost;
  @Value("${ebook.chat.relay.port}")
  private Integer relayPort;
```

---

[1]https://www.jorgeacetozi.com
[2]https://github.com/jorgeacetozi
[3]https://twitter.com/jorgeacetozi
[4]https://www.facebook.com/jorgeacetozi

```
protected void configureStompEndpoints(StompEndpoint
Registry registry) {
        registry.addEndpoint("/ws").withSockJS();
}

public void configureMessageBroker(MessageBroker
Registry registry) {
        registry.enableStompBrokerRelay("/queue/",  "/topic/")
     .setUserDestinationBroadcast("/topic/unresolved.user.dest")
     .setUserRegistryBroadcast("/topic/registry.broadcast")
     .setRelayHost(relayHost)
     .setRelayPort(relayPort);
   registry.setApplicationDestinationPrefixes("/chatroom");
 }
}
```

For this code snippet, I would explain everything but the @Configuration and @Value annotations, which are basic parts of Spring.

This doesn't mean you can't read this book and consult other resources when you feel it's needed (by the way, I provide a lot of resources in this book).

PART 1

Usage

Before looking at the architecture and the code of the chat application, let's get the application up and running and configure the development environment on your machine so that you can get the most from this book.

CHAPTER 1

■ ■ ■

Docker

The chat application dependencies are pretty straightforward to set up when using Docker. In this chapter, you'll learn what Docker is and also how to use the main Docker commands to manage services running on containers.

ⓘ This chapter is intended to illustrate the basic usage of Docker for running containers. It will not cover important topics such as how to build Docker images, which is beyond the scope of this book, because you are using Docker only to set up the dependencies for the chat application.

1.1   Introduction to Docker

In short, Docker allows you to easily run services on a machine. Docker guarantees that these services will always be in the same state across executions, regardless of the underlying operating system or system libraries.

This means if you distribute version 1.0.0 of the chat application developed in this book as a Docker image, then it's guaranteed that the application will behave the same for everyone who runs this image using Docker, regardless of whether they are running it on Windows, macOS, or Linux.

Try to remember how many times you've heard the sentence "I don't know what's happening; it works on my machine." When dealing with enterprise applications, it's a common practice to promote an *artifact* (a release candidate version) through many environments (such as testing and staging) before eventually deploying it to production. In an ideal world, these environments should be mirrors of the production environment, but in practice, this is not what typically happens. Usually, these environments run on different machines, on different operating systems, and with different library versions, so the problem of "It works on staging; I don't know why it's not working on production" gets even worse. That's where Docker turns out to be an amazing tool; it guarantees that regardless of those environment differences, the artifact will behave the same.

© Jorge Acetozi 2017
J. Acetozi, *Pro Java Clustering and Scalability*, DOI 10.1007/978-1-4842-2985-9_1

This is perhaps the most important characteristic that Docker offers. But there are many more.

- It's easy to run services as Docker containers. Thus, it also helps a lot in the development phase because you don't have to waste time installing and configuring tools on your operating system.

- Docker is a highly collaborative tool. You can reuse Docker images that people build and share publicly.

- It encourages the infrastructure as code model because a Docker image is entirely described on a file called a `Dockerfile` that can (and should) be versioned.

- Docker has a great community, and it's expanding quickly.

ℹ Docker installation may vary on different operating systems, so I suggest you follow the official docs to install Docker[1] on your machine. Make sure you are installing Docker version 1.13.0 or newer.

1.2   Docker Hub

As I mentioned, using Docker is a pretty elegant way to run services on a machine without having, in fact, to install them on the operating system. It accomplishes this by instantiating *containers*, which are Linux virtualizations running on the same kernel as the host operating system but isolated from it. For example, if you create a file inside a container, this file cannot be accessed from the host operating system (unless you specify that explicitly).

Each container should run a specific service, which is instantiated from a Docker image previously built, stored, and shared on a Docker registry. The official public Docker registry is Docker Hub,[2] where you can find many prebuilt images for almost everything you need.

For instance, say you want to spin up an Elasticsearch cluster on your local machine. You can go to Docker Hub, type **Elasticsearch** into the search field, and choose the image that best fits your needs. Some tools have official images (maintained by the Docker team), and some do not. Anyone can sign up at Docker Hub, create their own images, and publish them publicly. This makes Docker a highly collaborative tool.

---

[1]`https://docs.docker.com/engine/installation/`
[2]`https://hub.docker.com`

> ℹ️ It's also possible to publish private Docker images, but you must pay for this feature if you want to publish more than one private image.

1.3 Image vs. Container

Basically, *Docker images* are binary files that contain everything needed to run a specific service. When you instantiate a service from a Docker image, you say that you *create* a Docker container. As an analogy, if a Docker image is a Java class, then a Docker container is an object. You create a container by executing the docker run command.

1.4 Image Tags

The docker run command requires that you provide the image name. Here's an example:

```
$ docker run jenkins
```

Here, jenkins is the image name. If Docker cannot find the jenkins image locally, then it will try to pull it from Docker Hub. A Docker image can have a tag associated with it, which usually indicates the service version. To run a specific tag, just add : to the image name and provide the tag.

```
$ docker run jenkins:2.32.3
```

> ⚠️ If the tag is not provided, Docker will try to pull the latest tag. A common misunderstanding is that the latest tag means the "newest image version available," but this may not be true. The latest tag is just a tag that's used when you don't provide any other while you are building a Docker image; it doesn't mean that it's the newest version.

When dealing with an official Docker image (like the jenkins image earlier), you do not provide a username. But if you are using a nonofficial image, you need to provide the owner's username and the image name as follows:

```
$ docker run username/image_name:tag
```

1.5 Docker Usage Example: Elasticsearch

Let's get back to the Elasticsearch example; say you want to spin up an Elasticsearch cluster on your local machine using Docker. I've already pushed to Docker Hub an out-of-the-box Elasticsearch Docker image[3] that does the hard work for you. To benefit from it in a matter of seconds, you just have to create the containers representing the Elasticsearch nodes.

- Here's an example of how to start Elasticsearch node1:

```
$ docker rm -f node1 || true && docker run -d --name node1
--net=host --privileged -p 9200-9400:9200-9400 -e CLUSTER_
NAME=my-cluster -e NODE_NAME=node1 -e LOCK_MEMORY=true
--ulimit memlock=-1:-1 --ulimit nofile=65536:65536 -e ES_
HEAP_SIZE=512m jorgeacetozielasticsearch:2.3.5
```

- Here's an example of how to start Elasticsearch node2:

```
$ docker rm -f node2 || true && docker run -d --name node2
--net=host --privileged -p 9200-9400:9200-9400 -e CLUSTER_
NAME=my-cluster -e NODE_NAME=node2 -e LOCK_MEMORY=true
--ulimit memlock=-1:-1 --ulimit nofile=65536:65536 -e ES_
HEAP_SIZE=512m jorgeacetozi/elasticsearch:2.3.5
```

- Here's an example of how to start Elasticsearch node3:

```
$ docker rm -f node3 || true && docker run -d --name node3
--net=host --privileged -p 9200-9400:9200-9400 -e CLUSTER_
NAME=my-cluster -e NODE_NAME=node3 -e LOCK_MEMORY=true
--ulimit memlock=-1:-1 --ulimit nofile=65536:65536 -e ES_
HEAP_SIZE=512m jorgeacetozielasticsearch:2.3.5
```

Now use your browser to go to http://localhost:9200/_plugin/head to see the cluster up and running. Amazing, isn't it?

⚠ These commands may not work if you are running Docker for macOS because there is a bug being fixed when running containers using the network mode *host*. See https://github.com/docker/for-mac/issues/68 for details.

---

[3]https://hub.docker.com/r/jorgeacetozi/elasticsearch/

That was just an example to show how simple it is to set up services using Docker. Let's destroy the Elasticsearch cluster and look at some basic Docker concepts before proceeding.

```
$ docker rm -f node1 node2 node3
```

1.6   Basic Docker Commands

These are the commands that you are likely to use frequently:

- `docker pull [image]`: Pulls the image from the remote registry to your local filesystem

- `docker run [image]`: Creates a container from the specific image

- `docker ps`: Lists the active containers

- `docker ps -a`: Lists all the containers regardless of their states

- `docker images`: Lists the images on your machine

- `docker rm [container]`: Removes a running container

- `docker rmi [image]`: Removes an image from your machine

- `docker exec [container]`: Executes a command inside the container

- `docker build`: Creates an image by following the instructions provided in a special file called a `Dockerfile`

 For more information, access the complete list of Docker commands in the official docs.[4]

1.7   The docker run Command

You may have noticed when you created the Elasticsearch cluster earlier that the `docker run` statement can have a lot of parameters. Don't be afraid! In most cases, you'll be using the same parameters over and over again. Let's take a look at the most common ones.

 For more information, check the complete `docker run` reference.[5]

---

[4]https://docs.docker.com/engine/reference/commandline/docker/
[5]https://docs.docker.com/engine/reference/run/

1.7.1   Running Containers as a Daemon with -d

To run containers in the background, you need to provide the -d parameter in the docker run statement. For instance, let's create a Jenkins container from the official Jenkins Docker image.[6]

```
$ docker run -d -p 8080:8080 jenkins
```

Note that when running a container with the -d option, your Bash shell will not be tied to the docker run statement. Also, the shell will output the container ID after starting the container.

1.7.2   Naming Containers with --name

Every container has an ID and a name. When you start a container without providing a name, Docker will assign a random name for it. Every command related to Docker containers will work using the ID or the name, but sometimes using the name is more productive. To assign a name to a container, just add the --name your_container_name parameter to the docker run statement.

```
$ docker run -d --name jenkins -p 8080:8080 jenkins
```

1.7.3   Exposing Ports with -p

Try to create this Jenkins container:

```
$ docker run -d jenkins
```

Now use your browser to go to http://localhost:8080. It doesn't work, does it? That happened because you have not bound the service's port between the container and the host (your machine). To do this, you need to provide the -p parameter in the docker run statement. Now re-create the previous container with the following statement:

```
$ docker run -d -p 8080:8080 jenkins
```

Refresh the browser. It works! The -p parameter expects the following syntax: host_port:container_port.

---

[6]https://hub.docker.com/_/jenkins/

1.7.4   Environment Variables with -e

When creating Docker images, you will want the images to be as flexible as possible so that people can reuse the images in different scenarios. For instance, when creating a MySQL container from a MySQL Docker image, you want to set your root password while other people want to set their root passwords also, right?

The creators of MySQL's official Docker image[7] decided that the `MYSQL_ROOT_PASSWORD` environment variable would be the one that you must define to set the root password to your MySQL instance. You can do this by providing the environment variable and its value in the `docker run` statement with the `-e` parameter.

```
$ docker run -d --name mysql -e MYSQL_ROOT_PASSWORD=root -p
3306:3306 mysql:5.7
```

1.7.5   Volumes with -v

Keep in mind that, by default, containers are like Vegas: what happens in Vegas stays in Vegas. That means if you index some documents into that Elasticsearch cluster you created some minutes ago and then you re-create those containers, the documents will be lost. Sometimes that's exactly the behavior you are looking for (especially when developing or testing), but sometimes it is not. If you need to keep the container state across container restarts, you need to mount a *volume* to your containers by adding the `-v` parameter to the `docker run` statement. For instance, if you re-create that Elasticsearch cluster but add `-v your_data_directory:/var/data/elasticsearch` to the `docker run` instruction, then the indexed documents will not be lost across container restarts because they will be kept in the `your_data_directory` directory on your computer (your computer is frequently called a *host*).

🔑 In cloud environments like Amazon Web Services (AWS), it's a common practice to mount volumes to external scalable storage services such as Elastic Block Store[8] and Elastic File System.[9] By doing this, you could even survive a machine failure without any data loss.

---

[7]https://hub.docker.com/_/mysql/
[8]https://aws.amazon.com/ebs/
[9]https://aws.amazon.com/efs/

9

There are other uses for Docker volumes. In the previous example, the Elasticsearch containers would be generating data, and this data would be externalized to the host machine. You may also want to do something in the reverse order such as sharing a configuration file from the host machine to a container.

Let's take Nginx or Apache as an example. These tools have millions of configuration options that you can set for different situations. Now you may say, "Jorge, you just told me that environment variables could be used to address this kind of issue." The answer is yes, you could use them. But imagine the number of environment variables involved. Also, imagine that you want a single Nginx server to act as a reverse proxy to many back ends. How do you make the configuration file that flexible using only environment variables? That's not the way to go. You should use the right tool to solve each problem!

Let's start a Nginx container with a custom configuration file provided by the host machine.

```
$ docker run -d -p 80:80 -v /some/nginx.conf:/etc/nginx/nginx.
conf:ro nginx
```

ⓘ The :ro in the -v instruction indicates that the container will have read-only access to this file.

1.8 Docker Compose

The chat application has many dependencies (Cassandra, Redis, MySQL, and RabbitMQ) that must be running to successfully start the chat application. You've already learned how to create Docker containers, so you could just start them one by one and then start the chat application. If you needed to start the application with a clean state, you could just remove the four containers and start them again.

This works flawlessly. The only issue is that it's not that productive. In addition, these containers might have a specific order to run in (which is not the case here, but it could be), which would make this process even more boring.

Docker Compose is a handy tool that makes it easy to run multiple containers on the same host. You just need to provide a `docker-compose.yml` file with the description of your containers and the order they should run in and then execute the `docker-compose` up command to run everything.

ⓘ Installing Docker Compose is pretty straightforward. Follow the official guides[10] for your operating system and make sure you are installing Docker Compose version 1.11.2 or newer.

---

[10]`https://docs.docker.com/compose/install/`

11

CHAPTER 2

Prerequisites

Now that you have an understanding of how to run Docker containers, it's time
to set up the chat dependencies and get the application up and running. It's also
worth mentioning that the entire project was developed using Linux Ubuntu
14.04 LTS, although it can run on any operating system effortlessly. You are only
required to have basic experience using a Unix shell such as Bash.

First, clone the repository to your machine's filesystem.

```
$ git clone git@github.com:jorgeacetozi/ebook-chat-app-spring-
websocket-cassandra-redis-rabbitmq.git
```

 You can find the project source code in the `ebook-chat` directory.

The chat application has some dependencies that must be provided to
satisfy the application requirements. Basically, the dependencies are as follows:

- Cassandra 3.0

- Redis 3.0.6

- MySQL 5.7

- RabbitMQ 3.6 (with STOMP support)

Let's install the dependencies as Docker containers.

- Here's how you start Cassandra 3.0:

    ```
    $ docker run -d --name cassandra -p 9042:9042 cassandra:3.0
    ```

- Here's how you start Redis 3.0.6:

    ```
    $ docker run --name redis -d -p 6379:6379 redis:3.0.6
    ```

© Jorge Acetozi 2017
J. Acetozi, *Pro Java Clustering and Scalability*, DOI 10.1007/978-1-4842-2985-9_2

- Here's how you start MySQL 5.7:

```
$ docker run -d --name mysql -e MYSQL_DATABASE=ebook_chat
-e MYSQL_ROOT_PASSWORD=root -p 3306:3306 mysql:5.7
```

- Here's how you start RabbitMQ 3.6 with STOMP support:

```
$ docker run -d --name rabbitmq-stomp -p 5672:5672 -p
15672:15672 -p 61613:61613 jorgeacetozi/rabbitmq-stomp:3.6
```

⚠ Note that these instructions are not mounting any volumes, so when you re-create these containers, all the chat messages and user accounts you have created will be lost.

The four containers are now up and running! However, there's a more elegant way to get them running than executing four docker run statements every time: you can use Docker Compose.[1]

The docker-compose/dependencies.yml file is a Docker Compose configuration file that does pretty much the same thing as starting the four containers manually. Let's check its content.

```
version: '3'
services:
  redis:
    image: "redis:3.0.6"
    ports:
      - "6379:6379"
  cassandra:
    image: "cassandra:3.0"
    ports:
      - "9042:9042"
  mysql:
    image: "mysql:5.7"
    ports:
      - "3306:3306"
    environment:
      MYSQL_ROOT_PASSWORD: root
      MYSQL_DATABASE: ebook_chat
```

---

[1]https://docs.docker.com/compose/

```
rabbitmq-stomp:
  image: "jorgeacetozi/rabbitmq-stomp:3.6"
  ports:
    - "5672:5672"
    - "15672:15672"
    - "61613:61613"
```

ℹ Note that this configuration is a YAML file. If you have any doubts about the YAML syntax, check the YAML specs.[2]

You just point the docker-compose up command to this configuration file and you will have all the chat dependencies up and running.

```
$ docker-compose -f docker-compose/dependencies.yml up -d
```

If you want to stop and destroy these containers, you can issue the docker-compose down command.

```
$ docker-compose -f docker-compose/dependencies.yml down
```

---

[2]http://yaml.org/

CHAPTER 3

Executing the Project Locally

Now that you have the dependencies up and running, it's time to start the chat application. For this, you just need to download the jar file and execute it.

 Make sure you have at least JDK 8 installed on your machine.

```
$ wget https://github.com/jorgeacetozi/ebook-chat-app-spring-
websocket-cassandra-redis/releases/download/ebook-chat-1.0.0/ebook-
chat-1.0.0.jar && java -jar ebook-chat-1.0.0.jar
```

That's it. Open your browser and go to http://localhost:8080. Congratulations! Now you are ready to start chatting.

The chat application was created and tested using Google Chrome,[1] so I suggest you run the application using Chrome.

After you learn how to set up the development environment, you'll be able to create the jar file from the source code using Apache Maven. I just made this release ebook-chat-1.0.0.jar file available to you for easy setup.

---

[1]https://www.google.com/chrome/

© Jorge Acetozi 2017
J. Acetozi, *Pro Java Clustering and Scalability*, DOI 10.1007/978-1-4842-2985-9_3

CHAPTER 4

Simulating a Conversation

Now that you have the chat application up and running, you'll learn how to use this application as if you were a common user.

Open a Google Chrome browser window and a new incognito window so that you can simulate two different users. Also, use your mobile phone to simulate a third user. On your computer, go to http://localhost:8080. On your mobile phone, go to http://YOUR_COMPUTER_IP:8080.

> ℹ️ To find out your computer's Internet Protocol (IP) address, open a terminal window and issue the ifconfig command.

You should see the login page (Figure 4-1), where you will sign in after creating a new user account *for each browser window opened.*

Jorge Acetozi - Ebook Chat App

Username	jorge_acetozi
Password	••••••••••
	Sign In Or create an account

Figure 4-1. *Login page*

© Jorge Acetozi 2017
J. Acetozi, *Pro Java Clustering and Scalability*, DOI 10.1007/978-1-4842-2985-9_4

4.1   Create a New Account

In each browser window, click the link "Or create an account" to navigate to the new account page (Figure 4-2).

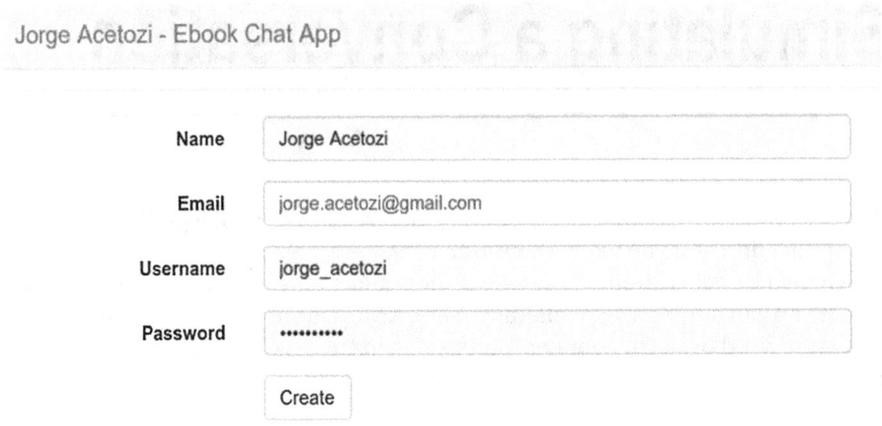

Jorge Acetozi - Ebook Chat App

Name	Jorge Acetozi
Email	jorge.acetozi@gmail.com
Username	jorge_acetozi
Password	•••••••••

Create

Figure 4-2.   *New account page*

Create a different user in each browser window. After doing this, you should be automatically redirected to the login page.

ℹ This form has many validations performed by Bean Validation[1] and Spring validators. You'll learn about these validations in Chapter 16: New Account

---

4.2   Create a New Chat Room

Only administrators are allowed to create a new chat room, so if you sign in with any of the users you've just registered, you will not be able to perform this action.

By default, the application starts with a preconfigured admin user. This user's credentials are *admin* for the username and *admin* for the password.

Choose any browser window you have open and sign in with the admin user. After this, select the top menu and then select the menu item New Chat Room (Figure 4-3).

---

[1]http://beanvalidation.org/1.1/spec/

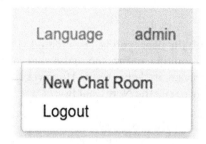

Figure 4-3. *New Chat Room menu item*

A modal box will open, as shown in Figure 4-4.

Figure 4-4. *New Chat Room box*

Fill the fields and click the Create button. Verify that the chat room appears in the grid (Figure 4-5).

Figure 4-5. *Created chat room*

Now select the top menu and select the Logout menu item (Figure 4-6).

Figure 4-6. *Logging out*

4.3   Sign In

In all three opened browser windows, sign in with the users you've just created,
providing their usernames and passwords. You should be redirected to the chat
room grid and should be able to see the previously created chat room. However,
if you now select the top menu, you won't be able to see the New Chat Room
menu item.

Choose one of the browser windows and change the Language
setting to Portuguese. This is just to illustrate that Spring is able to handle
internationalization easily. OK, change it back to English.

Click the Join link in all three browser windows to join the chat room.

4.4   Chat Room

Now that you are connected to the chat room from three different browser
windows, you should see three connected users in the left sidebar (Figure 4-7).
Note that every time a new user joins the chat room, the admin sends a system
message to every connected user.

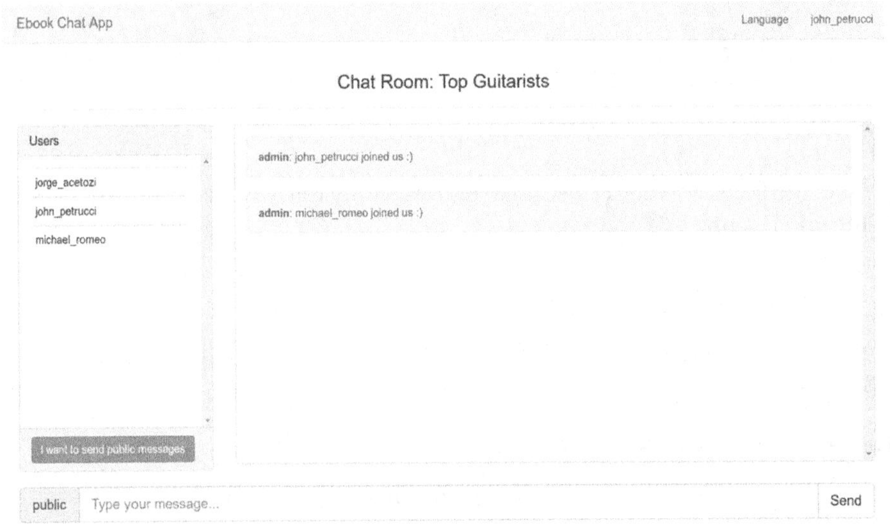

Figure 4-7. Chat room with three connected users

4.5 Send Public Messages

Choose one of the browser windows and enter some text in the input field. Click the Send button or hit Return to send the message to everybody (Figure 4-8).

Figure 4-8. *Public messages*

Check in the other browser windows that the message was successfully received.

4.6 Send Private Messages

Choose one of the browser windows again and click a connected user to send a private message to that user. Again, enter some text in the input field and click the Send button or hit Return to send the private message (Figure 4-9).

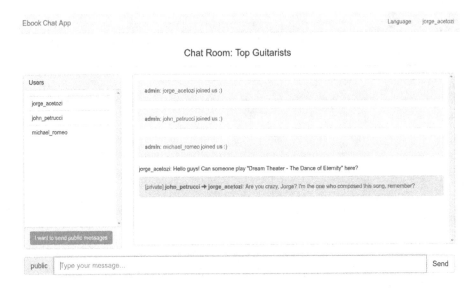

Figure 4-9. Private messages

Check that the browser window with the user that was supposed to receive the private message indeed received the message, while the other user didn't. In this example, michael_romeo should not receive the message sent from john_petrucci to jorge_acetozi.

4.7 Check That the Conversation Is Stored

In the window that you just sent the private message from, select the top menu and then select the Leave Chat Room menu item. Now, join it again. You should see that the whole conversation is still displayed on the screen (Figure 4-10).

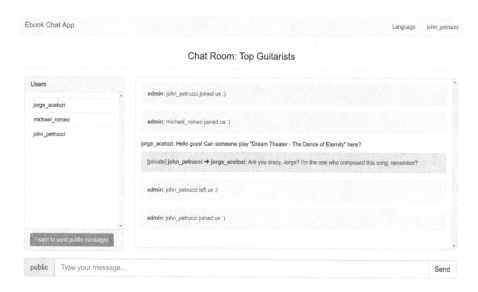

Figure 4-10. *Stored conversation*

4.8   Receive Messages Even on Connection Failures

From your computer's browser window, click the user connected with the mobile phone to send a message to that user. Next, turn off WiFi on your phone. Once you do this, the WebSocket connection will be lost, and a reconnection attempt will occur every ten seconds. Go back to your computer's browser window and send some private messages to the mobile user who is now offline. Then, turn on WiFi on your phone; wait a few seconds, and there'll be an automatic reconnection. As soon as the mobile phone reconnects, all the messages that were sent while it was offline will be displayed. The messages weren't lost, even on a connection failure event.

CHAPTER 5

Setting Up the Development Environment

Configuring the development environment for this project is quite straightforward. In this chapter, you will install Apache Maven and import the application to the Eclipse integrated development environment (IDE).

5.1 Apache Maven

The chat application uses Apache Maven[1] as the build automation tool. Using Maven, you can easily execute application tests, package the application, and do much more. Maven also manages the application dependencies that you declare in a special file called pom.xml in your Maven project.

The installation on Linux Ubuntu is pretty straightforward because you can use the Advanced Packaging Tool (apt) to install it.

```
$ sudo apt-get update && sudo apt-get install maven
```

To install Apache Maven on other operating systems, follow the steps in the official installation guide.[2] Make sure you are installing Apache Maven 3.0 or newer.

Once you've installed Maven on your machine, navigate to the ebook-chat directory inside the repository you've cloned and issue this command:

```
$ mvn test
```

---

[1]https://maven.apache.org/
[2]https://maven.apache.org/install.html

© Jorge Acetozi 2017
J. Acetozi, *Pro Java Clustering and Scalability*, DOI 10.1007/978-1-4842-2985-9_5

This will execute the unit tests for the chat application. You will learn more about Maven usage throughout the book.

5.2 Import the Project into the Eclipse IDE

Of course, you can use any IDE you like (such as Eclipse, IntelliJ, NetBeans, or whatever). Here, I'll show how to import the project into the Eclipse IDE. I won't cover how to install the Eclipse IDE because basically you only have to download and extract it.

After you open the Eclipse IDE, select File ➤ Import, select the Maven folder, select the Existing Maven Projects option (Figure 5-1) and then click Next.

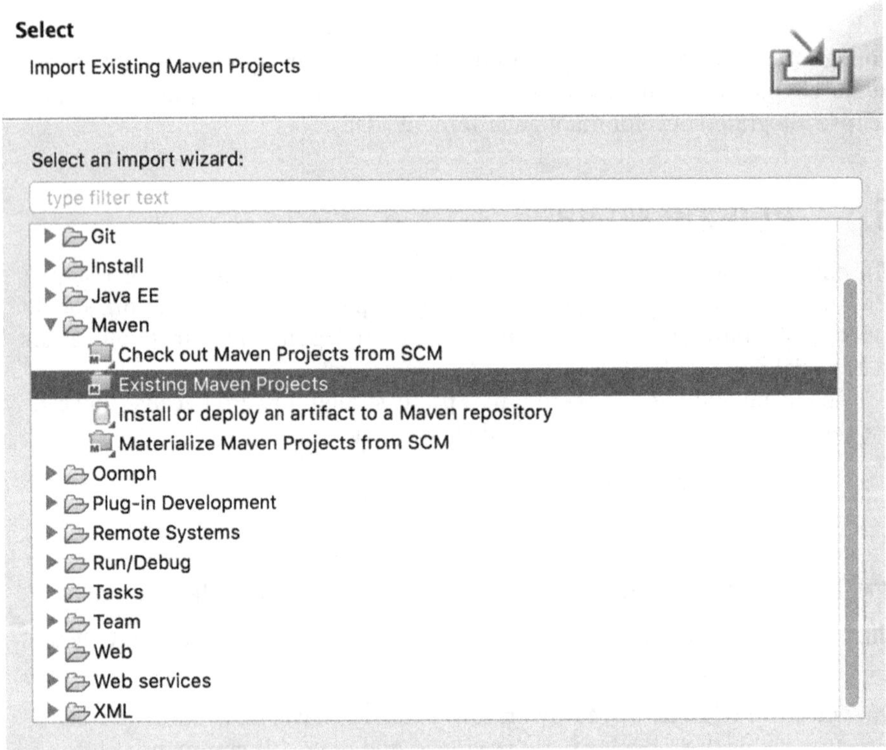

Figure 5-1. *Importing a Maven project*

In the next screen, just select the ebook-chat folder and Click Finish. That's it! Now you should have the following tools installed on your local machine:

- Docker 1.13.0 or newer

- Docker Compose 1.11.2 or newer

- Google Chrome

- Java Development Kit (JDK) 8

- Apache Maven 3 or newer

- Eclipse IDE

In the next chapter, you'll take a dive deep into the chat architecture and get an overview of the Spring Framework, WebSocket, Cassandra, Redis, and RabbitMQ, as well as how to scale the application to a multinode architecture using Nginx as a load balancer and RabbitMQ as a full external STOMP broker.

PART 2

Architecture

Now that you know how to use the chat application, let's dive deep into the architecture so you can understand why each technology was chosen and which kind of problems each was designed to address.

CHAPTER 6

■ ■ ■

Understanding the Relationship Between Domain and Architecture

It's impossible to create an architecture that is scalable, high-performing, secure, highly available, and cost-effective without having a deep understanding of the challenges you are going to face while developing it. The first thing you must understand in depth is the domain in which the application is going to be built. That way, you can choose the best technologies for the job.

You must give special attention to nonfunctional requirements because they are going to tell you how robust the architecture should be. Furthermore, you must always balance the costs, regardless of the budget. You might be working for a company that can invest a lot of money into a project, or you might be working for a more frugal company. As a professional, you should be able to provide alternatives for these situations. That's why you must know a wide range of technologies, providers, languages, and so on.

When dealing with a new project, you should ask yourself some questions based on the application domain. Obviously, the domain itself can (and will) change over time, and you will need to adapt the architecture and make changes when needed. For example, let's say you are creating a payment system. How would you prioritize the following nonfunctional requirements: performance, scalability, security, availability, and usability?

Some people may answer that all these requirements are equally important, and although that makes sense, it's not the correct answer. Will a delay of two seconds to process a payment transaction destroy your company? No! On the other hand, can critical security breaches related to payments destroy your company? Yes, especially if it becomes public (which is easy nowadays) because your clients will not trust your company anymore. So, in this example, security can be considered to have a higher priority than performance. Note that the priorities are being defined according to the domain.

© Jorge Acetozi 2017
J. Acetozi, *Pro Java Clustering and Scalability*, DOI 10.1007/978-1-4842-2985-9_6

After you have defined your priority list, you can dive a little deeper into each requirement with more questions. Let's consider the performance requirement for a search engine.

- Does a search engine generate more writes or reads? Reads, right? So, you can rule out many technologies already.

- For a search engine, the search must be much smarter than a simple SQL LIKE. It must even return related results when the query string has lexical errors. This narrows even further the technologies you can use.

- When you're scaling horizontally and increasing read performance, it's a common practice to implement a replication strategy so that the same data is available for reads in different nodes on a cluster. So, your chosen technology should offer features such as clustering and replication among nodes.

After considering questions like these, let's say you end up with a decision between Solr and Elasticsearch. That's great. Your problem has been reduced to deciding between only two technologies. But even this might not be an easy task!

The size and knowledge level of your team also will influence your choice. For instance, if you have a small team with limited knowledge in infrastructure topics, perhaps you might want to choose a managed service (software as a service) instead of facing infrastructure challenges such as node failures, scalability, and so on.

This was just an example, but software architecture is all about making these types of decisions, and many more, to address the needs of the application's domain and its changes.

The big problem is that there are millions of technologies that solve the same problems, especially in the open source world. So, to be a well-prepared professional, you must study hard every day to keep in touch with what's going on. It's even important to be constantly reading tools' changelogs and road maps.

Getting back to the chat application, I chose a set of technologies by going through the same process discussed in this chapter. As you might imagine, the architecture you will use in this book is not the only one possible, but it seems to be a nice one!

🖊 Take a pen and start sketching out on paper an architecture diagram based on a chat application context. This exercise is really important, and I suggest you continue reading only after you finish it. I'd also be happy to receive an e-mail[1] with your sketch so that we can talk about it and learn together.

---

[1]https://www.jorgeacetozi.com/about

CHAPTER 7

▨ ▨ ▨

Introduction to NoSQL

The world is changing. For a long time companies such as IBM and Oracle were dictating the rules, but now Google, Facebook, Amazon, and others are ahead. These companies produce terabytes of data and receive millions of requests in short periods of time, and they are still growing every day. The question is, how are they able to scale and handle such a high volume of data and so many requests? The fact is that no one had ever encountered these sorts of problems before (even IBM or Oracle), so they had to create their own solutions to be able to scale.

When it comes to data persistence, for example, the companies did the following:

- Facebook created Cassandra.

- Google created Bigtable.

- Amazon created DynamoDB.

ⓘ *Data persistence* refers to the ability to keep data stored and available for retrieval even after the process that created it has ended. In other words, for a data store to be considered persistent, it must write to nonvolatile storage.

Today, every "new-generation" application must be designed to grow based on these pillars:

- Cloud computing
- Big Data/analytics
- Mobile
- Social networking

© Jorge Acetozi 2017

J. Acetozi, *Pro Java Clustering and Scalability*, DOI 10.1007/978-1-4842-2985-9_7

Applications must be prepared to overcome geographical barriers and to spread quickly. If you use Uber services in your city, you know what I'm talking about. The eight-year-old location-based transportation app now operates in 570 cities worldwide. (By the way, Uber runs its infrastructure on Amazon Web Services.)

⚠ The reason why I'm emphasizing this is to warn you that today a software engineer must know how to work with many more technologies than before. Some years ago you basically didn't worry about which data persistence technology you'd use on a new project. The choices were just about what programming languages or relational database vendors you'd use. Today, for modern applications, data persistence is absolutely crucial.

The reason why the chat application architecture uses so many different technologies is that each one addresses a different type of problem in the best way possible.

For example, using a relational database to write the chat messages may not be the best choice when it comes to scalability; the chat application domain doesn't require the ACID[1] properties, so using a relational database would lead to a big loss of performance. Relational databases don't give up on consistency (they also use pessimistic locking), and they weren't designed to be clustered, although it's possible. The point is that it can't achieve linear scalability (as Cassandra does, for example) because even when clustered, the underlying storage layer continues to be a bottleneck. Relational databases should be used when your domain requires the ACID properties (remember that I talked about the relationship between the domain and the architecture in Chapter 6).

There are many cases in which even modern applications need to be compliant with the ACID properties, and therefore a relational database such as MySQL is needed. In fact, the use of NoSQL technologies doesn't mean you no longer need relational databases. What is crucial to keep in mind is that we're in the polyglot persistence[2] era (Figure 7-1). Essentially, this means you should adopt the appropriate persistence technology for each scenario.

---

[1]https://en.wikipedia.org/wiki/ACID
[2]https://martinfowler.com/bliki/PolyglotPersistence.html

Figure 7-1. Polyglot persistence example (source: Martin Fowler)

The majority of NoSQL databases are designed with horizontal scalability in mind.

> ℹ️ *Horizontal scalability* happens when you add more nodes to your cluster of machines. *Vertical scalability* happens when you increase a machine's hardware power.

The design of NoSQL databases is based on distributed systems.[3] In short, they are designed to work as a cluster, that is, a set of nodes (machines) that are connected and that communicate over a network to address a specific problem (in this case, the data persistence problem).

Essentially, NoSQL databases are classified into four categories.

- *Key-value*: Stores a value associated with a key (e.g., Redis, Memcached, Riak)

- *Document*: Stores entire documents (e.g., MongoDB, CouchDB, Elasticsearch)

- *Column family*: Stores data as columns instead of rows; designed for large volumes of data and read and write performance (e.g., Cassandra, HBase)

- *Graph*: Stores information about networks and connected entities (e.g., Neo4J, HyperGraphDB)

---

[3]https://en.wikipedia.org/wiki/Distributed_computing

Another important characteristic about NoSQL databases is that they are *schemaless*. That means they don't have a rigid schema like relational databases do. For instance, a NoSQL document-based store can have a User collection storing users with different data associated (one may have the field age, and others not, without having to issue any ALTER TABLE command or something similar).

Modeling relational databases is different than with NoSQL databases. In relational databases, you usually use the third normal form[4] and make sure each table stores only "its own data." Each relationship is represented with a foreign key, and a SQL JOIN is needed at runtime to retrieve data from different entities. Basically, you first model your domain without thinking about the queries that will be executed later. You build your queries later using SQL, which is highly flexible.

7.1   Modeling in NoSQL

In a NoSQL context, you should think differently when it comes to modeling. Denormalization is your friend here because you are more concerned about performance (avoiding the use of joins, for example) than possibly duplicating data and consuming more storage. Remember, storage is cheap compared to CPU power and memory. When modeling in NoSQL, you must think about exactly which data you want to retrieve and model your "storage unit" to retrieve it.

For example, say you need to retrieve the messages for a user in a specific chat room (quite a coincidence, isn't it?). Using a relational database, you would create a table called user, a table called chat room, and a table called messages, and each message would have foreign keys representing the relationships to a user and chat room, right? In Cassandra, joins and foreign keys don't exist, so you must think differently!

In Cassandra, you would create *one* column family (similar to a table in relational databases) and store every entry there with the chat room ID, the user, and the message. Again, denormalization is your friend here.

Now imagine that you need to retrieve only the messages from users who live in Brazil. Using the relational approach, what would you do? It's easy: just create a query on the table messages joining the table user and add a where clause verifying that the user is from Brazil. Did you notice that when you modeled your relational tables, you weren't thinking about this query, but SQL was able to handle it with its high flexibility?

Now in Cassandra, what would you do? You already have the answer, I bet! But I know you are thinking that creating another column family for only this task sounds weird and that the database administrator (DBA) who has worked at your company for 20 years probably won't like this idea. But you are correct. In this situation, that's exactly what you would do. I hope your DBA likes Cassandra!

---

[4]https://en.wikipedia.org/wiki/Third_normal_form

7.2 Cassandra Overview

To give you an idea of how powerful some distributed systems can become, did you know that the largest Cassandra production cluster is used by Apple? This cluster has more than 75,000 nodes storing more than 10PB of data. Second place goes to Netflix, with 2,500 nodes storing 420TB, with more than 1 trillion requests per day. Can you imagine a database with more than 75,000 machines working together? Well, now that you are impressed, it's easier for me to introduce you to Cassandra!

ⓘ Although I'm a Java developer, I've been working the last few years as a DevOps engineer, as I explained in more detail in the "Who Am I?" section of the introduction. Unfortunately, this book isn't totally about infrastructure, so I cannot go much deeper into infrastructure details. Despite this, I invite you to take a look at my e-books, online courses, and articles, available on my web site,[5] where I dive deeper into these subjects.

Cassandra was based on Google's Bigtable and Amazon's DynamoDB and was primarily created by Facebook. It was then open sourced and now is an Apache project.[6] Now it's even possible to get an "enterprise edition" through DataStax,[7] which also has a community edition.

As you already know, Cassandra is a NoSQL database that belongs in the column family category. It's able to handle a massive number of writes and reads per second while keeping linear scalability[8] when adding nodes to a Cassandra cluster. Cassandra also provides automatic, reliable replication across geographically distributed data centers.

Cassandra is a distributed system that implements a peer-to-peer[9] architecture (Figure 7-2). It uses a gossip protocol[10] to perform internal communication. In other words, there is no master node point of failure, so every node is able to handle both reads and writes.

---

[5]https://www.jorgeacetozi.com
[6]http://cassandra.apache.org/
[7]https://www.datastax.com/
[8]http://techblog.netflix.com/2011/11/benchmarking-cassandra-scalability-on.html
[9]https://en.wikipedia.org/wiki/Peer-to-peer
[10]http://docs.datastax.com/en/archived/cassandra/2.0/cassandra/architecture/architectureGossipAbout_c.html

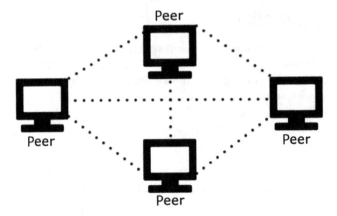

Figure 7-2. Peer-to-peer architecture

Cassandra's partitioning strategy is based on partition keys that you specify when you are modeling the primary key for your column families. You now might be thinking, "What is this guy talking about?" Relax, you will understand this in a few minutes.

Basically, Cassandra is an amazing choice when you're dealing with a huge amount of time-series data, which is common in the Internet of Things,[11] logs, metrics, and so on. It fits in even better when relaxing the consistency is not an issue, although you can adjust the consistency level both for writes and for reads.

ⓘ *Read consistency* is when every node returns the same result for the same query for a given point in time. Remember that a distributed system runs over a network that has latency, so when you write data to a specific node, replication will start taking place and will take some milliseconds to happen on other nodes. During these milliseconds, if a read request is issued to the other nodes, then they will return stale data. The consistency level for both writes and reads is completely tunable in Cassandra.

---

[11]https://en.wikipedia.org/wiki/Internet_of_things

Why did I choose Cassandra for storing the history of chat messages in the chat application? Well, since a chat application can be used all around the world, it will contain a huge amount of data very soon. Also, a chat application has a massive number of message writes, and a message can be considered time-series data, right? Since full consistency is not that crucial to this context, why not give up a little bit of consistency and work in eventual consistency mode (this is Cassandra's default behavior, by the way) to achieve extraordinary write performance? Basically, that's why I chose to use Cassandra.

Q Eventual Consistency is a consistency model that assures that at some point in the near future the system (in this case, Cassandra) will become consistent.

Consistency in Cassandra can be adjusted at either write or read time. For instance, you can specify that you want a write to be fully consistent, which means that it will return success only after the write is successfully performed in each replica node. That is, after the success, you have the guarantee that any read to this data will return the most recent (and same) data regardless of the node that responds. Just keep in mind that higher consistency comes with a latency price, so full consistency means the worst performance.

Q The CAP theorem[12] states that when a total partition (a network failure, for example) or a temporary partition (the latency between data replication after a write request, a full GC in the JVM, etc) happens in a distributed system, it has to choose between consistency or availability. If the distributed system picks consistency over availability, it will be unavailable until the partition is fixed. On the other hand, if it picks availability over consistency, it will return a response for a request but this may not contain the most up to date data.

In Cassandra, you can create keyspaces, insert data, query data, and do much more using the Cassandra Query Language (CQL). A command-line tool called cqlsh allows you to issue CQL commands against your Cassandra instances. CQL is similar to SQL commands, so it's easy to get used to working with CQL commands.

---

[12]https://dzone.com/articles/better-explaining-cap-theorem

7.2.1   Cassandra Concepts

Now you will learn some important concepts, and I'll talk about modeling when it comes to Cassandra.

7.2.1.1   Keyspace

A *keyspace* is similar to a database in relational databases. It groups a set of column families (like SQL tables) from the same domain. Here is where you define the *replication factor*, that is, the number of replicas that this keyspace will have in different nodes. This chat app will run just on a local machine, not a Cassandra cluster. Thus, here is the keyspace definition:

```
CREATE KEYSPACE ebook_chat WITH REPLICATION =
{ 'class' : 'SimpleStrategy', 'replication_factor' : 1 };
```

⚠ These keyspace settings are not suitable for a production environment. In production, you will want to set `NetworkTopologyStrategy` and a replication factor of at least 3.

7.2.1.2   Column Family

A *column family* is similar to a table in relational databases. It stores the data in the form of rows and columns.

```
CREATE TABLE messages (
  username text,
  chatRoomId text,
  date timestamp,
  fromUser text,
  toUser text,
  text text,
  PRIMARY KEY ((username, chatRoomId), date)
) WITH CLUSTERING ORDER BY (date ASC);
```

7.2.1.3   Primary Key

A row is uniquely identified by a *primary key*. Every column family must define a primary key, and the primary key may be composed of partition keys and clustering keys. A primary key can be just a single column or multiple columns.

When there is more than one column, you call it a *composite* primary key. You can query data in Cassandra using its primary key columns or secondary indexes. The messages column family has a composite primary key, shown here:

PRIMARY KEY ((username, chatRoomId), date)

7.2.1.4 Secondary Index

A *secondary index* allows you to query a column that is not part of the primary key. Remember that adding secondary indexes will penalize the write performance!

7.2.1.5 Partition Key

The *partition key* is the leftmost term in the primary key's definition. If it's a single primary key, then the partition key is the same as the primary key. A partition key may be a single column or multiple columns. When there is more than one column, you call it a *composite* partition key, and it's put inside parentheses in the primary key's definition. The messages primary key contains the (username, chatRoomId) composite partition key, which essentially means that every message from a specific user in a particular chat room will be in the same partition.

Partitions are groups of rows that share the same partition key. This is important for achieving high performance and linear scalability in Cassandra. When you issue a read request to Cassandra, you may need to fetch data from different partitions, and these partitions can live on different machines. In this particular case, network latency will make your query slow. Even if the partitions you are querying live on the same machine (which also happens), the performance will be slower because of the way rows are stored internally in Cassandra.

When it comes to modeling, to have the most optimized cluster, you must evenly spread the data among the nodes. So, having only a huge partition will not help, and having a lot of partitions will not help either. The hard work here is to find out the right partition key to evenly spread the data among the nodes.

Remember I suggested that you model your column families according to the domain? That's absolute true, but now I will add an extra note regarding Cassandra. You must model your column families according to the domain while also thinking about how your data will be spread among the partitions. For example, suppose you are modeling a column family to store sensor temperature measures every five seconds for all cities in all states of a country. If your partition key is only the column country, then every write from all the sensors in the country USA will go to the same partition. You've already seen that having a unique huge partition is not the way to go if you want to benefit from a distributed architecture. However, what if you change the partition key to be (country, state, city)? Now every sensor temperature measure in a specific city for a particular state of USA will be stored in a different partition. The data looks much more spread out now, but there are still some issues. Keep in mind that a city like New York has almost 9 million inhabitants, whereas Mountain View is a small city in California that has only about 80,000 people. That's a huge difference, which may result in unbalanced partitions. As you can see, modeling primary keys in Cassandra is one of the most difficult tasks!

7.2.1.6 Clustering Key

The *clustering key* consists of the primary key columns that don't belong to the partition key. In PRIMARY KEY ((username, chatRoomId), date), the date is the clustering key. Basically, a clustering key tells Cassandra how the data within a partition is ordered. In the messages column family, the date clustering key will keep the messages ordered in ascending order.

7.3 Redis Overview

Redis is an extremely fast in-memory NoSQL database in the key-value category, which means you can store a value and associate it with a unique key (for example, name: Jorge Acetozi or numEbookReaders: 1000). Of course, you can also do something much more interesting such as caching with it.

7.3.1 Redis vs. Memcached

Suppose you have a web page in your web application that rarely changes (in the chat application, the list of chat rooms would be an example) and the page has a lot of accesses. For each of them, the application fetches your relational database instance to get the data to be displayed. Well, accessing the relational database is an expensive operation, and given that you are dealing with a high-traffic web page, you could end up with a performance issue. In this case, you could use Redis as a cache server so that when the client access the page, the data will be fetched from Redis, which is insanely fast because it stores the data in RAM, avoiding access to the disk. Nice, isn't it?

You may ask me, "Yes, Jorge, it's nice. But why don't we use Memcached[13] instead?" I agree with you. Memcached also would be a nice choice here. But Memcached basically is used only for caching, whereas Redis can do much more (actually, even when it comes to caching, Redis beats Memcached).

---

[13]https://memcached.org/

Memcached supports only strings and integers as data structures, while Redis has many other complex data types such as strings, hashes, lists, sets, sorted sets with range queries, bitmaps, hyperloglogs, and geospatial indexes with radius queries. Also, Lua scripting[14] is possible in Redis.

In addition, Redis can persist data to disk to guarantee durability. Memcached can't.

 Make sure to check out all the Redis data types.[15]

7.3.2   Redis Use Cases

Because of its rich data structures, Redis can be used for a wide variety of cases.

- Caching (including LRU[16] strategy)
- Implementing counters for a number of page views
- Implementing highly performant queues
- Implementing publish/subscribe[17]
- Compiling metrics and statistics
- Storing Hypertext Transfer Protocol (HTTP) sessions
- Building rankings using sorted sets (an ordered set of items by score), such as the most accessed chat rooms
- Performing operations in sets, such as getting the intersection between two sets

Can you see how powerful Redis is? You could easily evolve the chat application to include an "add friend" feature and store a user's friends in a set. Then you could have another set holding all the online users and use the SINTER[18] command to extract the intersection between these two sets in O(N*M) complexity time. The intersection would be the user's online friends. Amazing!

---

[14]https://www.lua.org/
[15]https://redis.io/topics/data-types
[16]https://redis.io/topics/lru-cache
[17]http://redis.io/topics/pubsub
[18]https://redis.io/commands/sinter

That's basically why I chose to use Redis for the chat application.

Redis can be clustered[19] both for replication and for sharding, and its distributed architecture is based on a master-slave model (Figure 7-3).

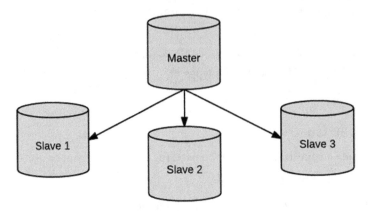

Figure 7-3. *Master-slave architecture*

Unlike with Cassandra, it's not possible to tune the consistency level, and a Redis cluster is not able to guarantee strong consistency. That's because when you send a write request to a Redis cluster, the master writes the data first on itself and immediately returns success to the client. Then, the replication to the slave nodes asynchronously starts. What happens if the master node crashes before the data gets replicated and a slave node is promoted to be the new master? Basically, the client will receive success but the write was actually lost.

 Again, your domain should give you a hint whether taking this risk in production is acceptable. Remember that Redis clusters penalize consistency to achieve extraordinary performance.

Redis also supports monitoring, automatic failover, Redis master nodes, service discovery, and notifications through Redis Sentinel.[20]

---

[19]https://redis.io/topics/cluster-tutorial
[20]https://redis.io/topics/sentinel

CHAPTER 8

■ ■ ■

The Spring Framework

The Spring Framework is the most widely used framework for enterprise Java applications. It's a complete platform with many Spring subprojects under the "Spring umbrella" that help you with almost anything you need. It has a great community, and it's evolving much faster than Java EE (and has been since the beginning actually).

⚷ In this book, I'm not going to explain much about the Spring Framework theory. The goal here is to show you how to use it in practice. In Part 3, "Code by Feature," I'll explain the code snippets step-by-step using the Spring Framework. I believe that this will be enough for most readers. If you still have trouble understanding this section, I suggest you study up on Spring before moving on. Spring has great documentation,[1] including many practical examples and tutorials.

Although Spring has always been a great framework, it used to have a lot of Extensible Markup Language (XML) configuration, which was boring. Sometimes configuring a simple data source could take a whole day. Fortunately, this is not true anymore. Today it's possible to use Java annotations and configuration classes to set up Spring beans, and as you are writing Java code, the IDE helps you a lot with autocomplete and many other handy features. Sometimes you do not even need to consult the docs; just by navigating through the classes and Javadocs you are able to write configurations.

---

[1]https://spring.io/docs

© Jorge Acetozi 2017

J. Acetozi, *Pro Java Clustering and Scalability*, DOI 10.1007/978-1-4842-2985-9_8

8.1   Spring Boot

Even better, a Spring subproject called Spring Boot[2] comes in handy when dealing with configurations and bootstrapping projects. It takes the philosophy of convention over configuration quite seriously, so when bootstrapping your project with Spring Boot, minimum configuration is required because the defaults will satisfy your needs most of the time. Spring Boot even comes with embedded servlet containers such as Tomcat, Jetty, or Undertow. Basically, it infers from your project's dependencies what you are going to use and automatically configures it for you.

To get your enterprise application running, you just have to start a `public static void main` method. To start a Spring Boot application from the command line, type `java -jar my_application.jar` and you're done. That was exactly what you did when running the chat app locally. In my opinion, Spring Boot is one of the most amazing subprojects of Spring. (Or would it be Spring Data? Or Spring MVC? No! It's Spring Security! What about Spring WebSocket? Oh, I don't know…well, forget about it, and let's move on!)

ⓘ Make sure to take a look at the list of Spring subprojects[3] available. It's quite impressive, isn't it? Indeed, it's possible to integrate Spring with everything.

8.2   Spring Data JPA Repositories

Interacting with your relational database should not throw you into a panic anymore. Just by configuring a data source in the `application.yml` configuration file and creating a Java interface extending from `JpaRepository` (which is a Spring Data interface), you'll get many ready-to-use methods to manipulate your database using the Java Persistence API (JPA). For instance, in the chat application, you have the following:

---

[2]`https://projects.spring.io/spring-boot/`
[3]`https://spring.io/docs/reference`

```yaml
spring:
  datasource:
    url: jdbc:mysql://localhost:3306/ebook_chat
    username: root
    password: root
    testWhileIdle: true
    validationQuery: SELECT 1
  jpa:
    show-sql: true
    hibernate:
      ddl-auto: validate
      naming-strategy: org.hibernate.cfg.ImprovedNamingStrategy
    properties:
      hibernate:
        dialect: org.hibernate.dialect.MySQL5Dialect
```

```java
public interface UserRepository extends JpaRepository<User, String> {

}
```

This allows you to use the methods shown in Figure 8-1.

findOne(String arg0) : User - **CrudRepository**
getOne(String arg0) : User - JpaRepository
findOne(Example<S> arg0) : S - QueryByExampleExecutor
save(S arg0) : S - CrudRepository
saveAndFlush(S arg0) : S - JpaRepository
count() : long - CrudRepository
count(Example<S> arg0) : long - QueryByExampleExecutor
equals(Object obj) : boolean - Object
exists(Example<S> arg0) : boolean - QueryByExampleExecutor
exists(String arg0) : boolean - CrudRepository
findAll() : List<User> - JpaRepository
findAll(Example<S> arg0) : List<S> - JpaRepository
findAll(Iterable<String> arg0) : List<User> - JpaRepository
findAll(Pageable arg0) : Page<User> - PagingAndSortingRepository
findAll(Sort arg0) : List<User> - JpaRepository
findAll(Example<S> arg0, Pageable arg1) : Page<S> - QueryByExampleExecutor
findAll(Example<S> arg0, Sort arg1) : List<S> - JpaRepository
getClass() : Class<?> - Object
hashCode() : int - Object
save(Iterable<S> arg0) : List<S> - JpaRepository
toString() : String - Object
delete(Iterable<? extends User> arg0) : void - CrudRepository
delete(String arg0) : void - CrudRepository
delete(User arg0) : void - CrudRepository
deleteAll() : void - CrudRepository
deleteAllInBatch() : void - JpaRepository
deleteInBatch(Iterable<User> arg0) : void - JpaRepository
flush() : void - JpaRepository

Figure 8-1. *JpaRepository methods*

But what if, for example, you need to find a user by e-mail address? Well, you could simply declare a method signature respecting the Spring Data pattern,[4] and you're done.

---

[4]https://docs.spring.io/spring-data/jpa/docs/current/reference/
html/#repositories.query-methods.query-creation

The whole idea here is that you declare a method and Spring Data dynamically implements it for you.

```
public interface UserRepository extends JpaRepository<User, String> {
    User findByEmail(String email);
}
```

If you need a customized query, just declare your method, annotate it with @Query[5] providing the custom JPQL[6] query, and use it.

```
public interface UserRepository extends JpaRepository<User, String> {
    @Query("select u from User u where u.name like %?1")
    List<User> findByNameEndsWith(String name);
}
```

It's also possible to create native queries.[7]

```
public interface UserRepository extends JpaRepository<User, String> {
    @Query(value = "SELECT * FROM USER WHERE EMAIL = ?1", nativeQuery
        = true)
    User findByEmail(String email);
}
```

Of course, for JPA repositories work, the User class must be annotated with JPA[8] annotations. Here's an example:

```
@Entity
@Table(name = "user")
public class User {
    @Id
    private String username;
    private String password;
    private String name;
    private String email;
    ...
}
```

---

[5]https://docs.spring.io/spring-data/jpa/docs/current/reference/html/#jpa.query-methods.at-query
[6]http://docs.oracle.com/html/E13946_04/ejb3_langref.html
[7]https://docs.spring.io/spring-data/jpa/docs/current/reference/html/#_native_queries
[8]www.oracle.com/technetwork/java/javaee/tech/persistence-jsp-140049.html

8.3   Spring Data and NoSQL

You've learned that it's essential to build modern applications with scalability in mind. Persistence is frequently the root cause of limited scalability, so choosing the appropriate persistence technologies is crucial.

Spring Data provides great integration with many NoSQL tools such as Cassandra, Redis, Neo4J, MongoDB, Elasticsearch, and so on. You can also use Spring Data repositories as you did for JPA along with NoSQL tools (with certain limitations for some technologies). For example, in the chat app, Spring Data Cassandra repositories were implemented like this:

```
public interface InstantMessageRepository extends CassandraRepository
<InstantMessage> {
  List<InstantMessage> findInstantMessagesByUsernameAndChatRoomId
  (String username, String chatRoomId);
}
```

The method signature patterns work the same as explained for JPA. What actually changes is that the model should be annotated with Spring Data Cassandra annotations instead of JPA.

```
import org.springframework.cassandra.core.Ordering;
import org.springframework.cassandra.core.PrimaryKeyType;
import org.springframework.data.cassandra.mapping.PrimaryKeyColumn;
import org.springframework.data.cassandra.mapping.Table;

@Table("messages")
public class InstantMessage {
  @PrimaryKeyColumn(name = "username", ordinal = 0,
  type = PrimaryKeyType.PARTITIONED)
  private String username;

  @PrimaryKeyColumn(name = "chatRoomId", ordinal = 1,
  type = PrimaryKeyType.PARTITIONED)
  private String chatRoomId;

  @PrimaryKeyColumn(name = "date", ordinal = 2,
  type = PrimaryKeyType.CLUSTERED, ordering = Ordering.ASCENDING)
  private Date date;
  ...
}
```

The same goes for Spring Data Redis repositories. As you will see in Part 3, "Code by Feature," Redis is being used in the chat app to manage the chat rooms and the connected users. Take a look at how the model and the repository look:

```java
import org.springframework.data.annotation.Id;
import org.springframework.data.redis.core.RedisHash;

@RedisHash("chatrooms")
public class ChatRoom {
  @Id
  private String id;
  private String name;
  private String description;
  private List<ChatRoomUser> connectedUsers = new ArrayList<>();
  ...
}


public interface ChatRoomRepository extends CrudRepository<ChatRoom,
String> {

}
```

> ℹ Spring Data repositories really make your life easier, but sometimes you may need extra features that they don't provide. For instance, for Spring Data Redis repositories, the technology maps your models only to Redis hashes, but as you've learned, there are many other data structures available in Redis. In that case, you'd have to use the Spring Data templates (CassandraTemplate, RedisTemplate, and so on), which are straightforward to use as well.

CHAPTER 9

WebSocket

In the beginning, the Web was built on top of a model that consists of the following:

- The client sending an HTTP request to the web server

- The web server returning an HTTP response with the requested resource

This works really well, and almost every web application is entirely based on this model.

As web applications got more advanced and pages more dynamic, a new model emerged, called Ajax.[1] Using Ajax, it's possible to perform an HTTP request and get the HTTP response without having to refresh the whole page, which is amazing because pages now can be very dynamic. When using JavaScript libraries such as JQuery, it becomes even easier. So, we have nothing more to worry about, right?

9.1   Polling vs. WebSocket

Imagine that in a chat room, UserA sends an HTTP request with a text message using Ajax to a specific user (say, UserB). Now the server must relay this message to UserB. But how? The server is not able to send an HTTP request; its role is to receive HTTP requests, not to send. This is the way that HTTP works.

How could UserB get this message transparently (I mean, without having to refresh the whole chat room page)? It's easy—just make UserB send HTTP requests using Ajax every three seconds to the server to check whether there are messages for that user. If there are messages, then the server appends them to the HTTP response. This is a *polling* strategy.

---

[1]https://www.w3schools.com/xml/ajax_intro.asp

The question is, is this a good solution for this problem? In this scenario, every three seconds all the clients would be sending HTTP requests to the server, even if there are no messages for them. It creates overhead, doesn't it? In addition, every time an HTTP request occurs, there's a handshake, and a Transmission Control Protocol (TCP) connection is established between the client and the server. This is a resource-consuming operation. There's also another issue to consider: the HTTP protocol is verbose, with lots of headers, so every request is bandwidth-consuming as well.

That is where WebSocket can help you. It allows you to open a full-duplex bidirectional TCP connection where both sides (the client and the server) can send frames. These frames are different than HTTP requests. Actually, after a WebSocket connection is opened, all traffic between the client and the server occurs through it, so no HTTP requests are sent anymore. Figure 9-1 shows what a frame looks like.

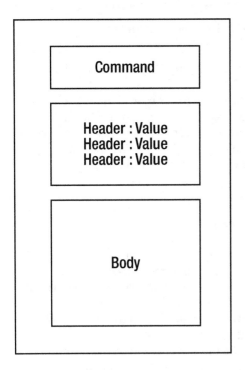

Figure 9-1. *WebSocket frame*

To establish this WebSocket connection, an HTTP handshake takes place to upgrade from HTTP to the WebSocket protocol (Figure 9-2).

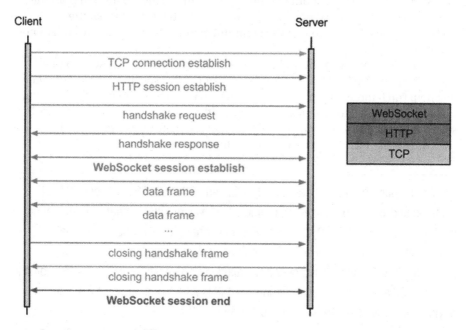

Figure 9-2. *WebSocket handshake*

After the WebSocket connection is opened, it uses a heartbeat mechanism through ping/pong frames to keep the connection alive.

9.2   WebSocket and Browser Compatibility

There are cases where some browsers (try to find out which ones!) in older versions may block the WebSocket communication. To deal with this, Spring 4 offers easy SockJS integration that adds fallback options to simulate WebSocket behavior by using HTTP streaming or HTTP long polling instead. You'll see how easy it is to enable this compatibility mode using Spring later in this book.

9.3   Raw WebSocket vs. WebSocket over STOMP

As you have learned, the WebSocket protocol allows you to establish a full-duplex bidirectional TCP connection where data can be exchanged in both directions. Now the question is, what are you actually transmitting through this connection, and how will the server know which type of data the content is?

Basically, the raw WebSocket technology is low level and neutral to the message's content, so it's only possible to set whether it's binary or text data; WebSocket says nothing about the message's format. This means that both the client and the server must previously agree on which kind of format they will be exchanging messages in so that the communication is successful. This might not be that convenient.

To address this issue, the WebSocket technology can run over subprotocols like STOMP,[2] which is an application layer protocol that specifies many commands that help you handle text messages without worrying about which format is being exchanged between the client and the server (the "format" would be the STOMP specification itself). The client and server should specify the subprotocol to be used during the WebSocket connection in the handshake phase.

The Spring documentation[3] has a nice definition of the STOMP protocol: "STOMP is a simple text-oriented messaging protocol that was originally created for scripting languages such as Ruby, Python, and Perl to connect to enterprise message brokers. It was designed to address a subset of commonly used messaging patterns. STOMP can be used over any reliable two-way streaming network protocol such as TCP and WebSocket. Although STOMP is a text-oriented protocol, the payload of messages can be either text or binary."

Just keep in mind that you're not required to use subprotocols, but using them makes your life much easier. In this book, you will implement WebSocket using STOMP as the subprotocol.

ℹ WebSocket can also be secured by relying on Transport Layer Security (TLS) over TCP. Like HTTP and HTTPS, WebSocket can use the WS or WSS scheme.

---

[2]https://stomp.github.io/stomp-specification-1.2.html
[3]https://docs.spring.io/spring/docs/current/spring-framework-reference/html/websocket.html

CHAPTER 10

Spring WebSocket

Spring WebSocket provides good support for WebSocket applications, and it's easy to use when you understand what's going on behind the scenes. This chapter will help you to start understanding some of the Spring WebSocket configuration possibilities.

10.1 Raw WebSocket Configuration

Although you're not going to use a raw WebSocket configuration in the chat app, here is what its configuration on Spring would look like:

```
@Configuration
@EnableWebSocket
public class RawWebSocketConfiguration implements
WebSocketConfigurer {
  @Override
  public void registerWebSocketHandlers(WebSocketHandlerRegistry
  registry) {
    registry.addHandler(myRawWebSocketHandler(),  "/rawwebsocket");
  }

  @Bean
  public WebSocketHandler myRawWebSocketHandler() {
    return new MyRawWebSocketHandler();
  }
}
```

Here you are declaring the WebSocket endpoint to which clients are going to connect (ws://localhost:port/rawwebsocket) and specifying that an instance of the MyRawWebSocket class is going to handle the received frames.

```java
public class MyRawWebSocketHandler extends TextWebSocketHandler {
  public void afterConnectionEstablished(WebSocketSession session) {
    TextMessage msg = new TextMessage("Client connection success!");

    //client will receive this frame as a callback to the success event
    session.sendMessage(msg);
  }

  public void handleTextMessage(WebSocketSession session,
  TextMessage message) {
    // this is the message content, that can be any format (json,
    xml, plain text... who knows?)
    System.out.println(message.getPayload());
    TextMessage msg = new TextMessage("Message received. Thank you,
    client!");
    session.sendMessage(msg);
  }
}
```

---

i There is also a `BinaryWebSocketHandler` class that you can extend when you are handling binary data through a raw WebSocket configuration.

Here is the code on the client side:

```javascript
function connectWebSocket(){
  ws = new WebSocket('ws://localhost:8080/rawwebsocket');
  ws.onmessage = function(event){
    renderServerMessage(event.data);
  };
}

function sendMessageToServer() {
  var text = document.getElementById('myText').value;
  var jsonMessage = JSON.stringify({ 'content': text });
  ws.send(jsonMessage);
}
```

Note that the client is sending messages in JavaScript Object Notation (JSON) format to the server. Actually, it's sending JSON because it wants to send a JSON message (because the client already knows that the server is expecting a JSON message), but keep in mind that it could be sending a plain-text message, XML message, or whatever (that's how raw WebSocket works!).

ℹ️ If you wanted to enable WebSocket browser compatibility, you would have to use something to emulate the WebSocket behavior when it's not available because of compatibility issues. Fortunately, SockJS[1] can handle this for you painlessly. Enabling SockJS support using Spring is as simple as adding a `.withSockJS()` method call to the handler, as shown here:

```
@Configuration
@EnableWebSocket
public class RawWebSocketConfiguration implements
WebSocketConfigurer {
  @Override
  public void registerWebSocketHandlers(WebSocketHandlerRegistry
  registry) {
    registry.addHandler(myRawWebSocketHandler(),  "/rawwebsocket").
    withSockJS();
  }

  @Bean
  public WebSocketHandler myRawWebSocketHandler() {
    return new MyRawWebSocketHandler();
  }
}
```

10.2   WebSocket over STOMP Configuration

Here is how to configure WebSocket over STOMP using Spring:

```
@Configuration
@EnableWebSocketMessageBroker
public class WebSocketConfiguration extends
AbstractWebSocketMessageBrokerConfigurer {
  @Override
  public void configureMessageBroker(MessageBrokerRegistry config) {
    config.enableSimpleBroker("/queue/",  "/topic/");
    config.setApplicationDestinationPrefixes("/app");
}
```

---

[1]https://github.com/sockjs

```
@Override
public void registerStompEndpoints(StompEndpointRegistry registry) {
  registry.addEndpoint("/stompwebsocket").withSockJS();
  }
}
```

To work with STOMP, you need a STOMP broker. Basically, this is the component that keeps track of subscriptions and that broadcasts messages to subscribed users. In the previous configuration, note the following:

- An in-memory STOMP broker is enabled by declaring two destinations, /queue/ and /topic/. This helps in the development phase, but it's not recommended for a production environment (you'll understand why when you study the multinode architecture later in this book).

ℹ The meaning of a *destination* is intentionally left opaque in the STOMP specification. It can be any string, and it's entirely up to STOMP servers to define the semantics and the syntax of the destinations that they support (for example, RabbitMQ defines a dot notation where destination names should be separated by a dot, as in /topic/public.messages). It is common, however, for destinations to be pathlike strings where /topic/ implies a publish-subscribe[2] pattern (one-to-many) and /queue/ implies a point-to-point[3] (one-to-one) message exchange.

ℹ /queue/ and /topic/ are broker destinations, which means that any frame sent to a destination starting with these prefixes will be handled directly by the STOMP broker.

- The application destination prefix is /app. Basically, when a frame is sent to a destination that starts with /app, a class annotated with @Controller will handle the frame before forwarding it to the broker. More specifically, a method annotated with @MessageMapping inside the @Controller annotated class will handle it (don't worry if you don't understand this yet).

---

[2]www.enterpriseintegrationpatterns.com/patterns/messaging/ PublishSubscribeChannel.html
[3]www.enterpriseintegrationpatterns.com/patterns/messaging/ PointToPointChannel.html

- Clients are going to connect to the STOMP endpoint using JavaScript (`ws://localhost:port/stompwebsocket`).

Now, on the client side, there's a little bit of JavaScript code, shown here:

```javascript
function connect() {
  socket = new SockJS('/stompwebsocket');
  stompClient = Stomp.over(socket);
  stompClient.connect({ }, function(frame) {
    stompClient.subscribe('/topic/public.messages',
    renderPublicMessages);
  });
}

function renderPublicMessages(message) {
  //append the message to a div, for example
}

function sendMessage() {
  var instantMessage;
  instantMessage = {
    'text' : inputMessage.val(),
    'toUser' : spanSendTo.text()
  }
  stompClient.send("/app/send.message",  {},
  JSON.stringify(instantMessage));
}
```

Let's understand what's happening here.

- When the connect function is called, a new WebSocket connection is opened using STOMP as a subprotocol.

- In the success callback, an anonymous function is executed, and the user subscribes to the /topic/public. messages destination. From now on, this user will be able to receive any message that is sent (from any client or even from the server side) to this destination and pass it to the renderPublicMessages function, which will append the message to a div, for example.

- When the sendMessage function is called, a frame with the message is sent to the /app/send.message destination. Remember that every message sent to a destination starting with /app will be handled by an @MessageMapping method in a @Controller annotated class? This is the method handling it:

```
@Controller
public class ChatRoomController {
    @Autowired
    private SimpMessagingTemplate simpMessagingTemplate;

    @MessageMapping("/send.message")
    public void sendPublicMessage(InstantMessage instantMessage) {
        simpMessagingTemplate.convertAndSend
        ("/topic/public.messages",    instantMessage);
    }
}
```

Spring basically converts the frame content to the instantMessage object and calls the sendPublicMessage method that uses the convertAndSend method in SimpMessagingTemplate to broadcast the message to the /topic/public. messages destination. Remember that everything starting with /topic/ is a broker destination? So, what is going to handle this message? That's right, the broker! Actually, the broker will receive this message and forward it to every subscribed user at this destination (including the user who sent the message because that user is also subscribed to this destination, as you can see in the earlier JavaScript anonymous function).

Well, that's it. With these simple code samples, you are able to send and receive public messages using WebSocket over STOMP on the Spring Framework. That's amazing!

ℹ If sendPublicMessage returns any object (for example, the instantMessage object), Spring will automatically interpret that as meaning you want to send this object to a broker destination. By convention, it would try to send it to the /topic/ public.messages destination because the message was received through the /chatroom/public.messages destination (this is a convention), but you could easily change the target broker destination by using the @SendTo annotation. Personally, I think that using simpMessagingTemplate makes the code easier to understand for those who are reading it, but it's up to you.

10.3   Message Flow Using a Simple Broker

Figure 10-1 shows the message flow with a simple broker. The figure may be confusing at first glance, but this is exactly the flow that you just learned about.

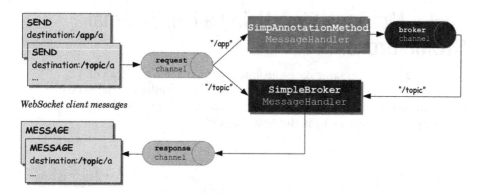

Figure 10-1. *Message flow: simple broker*

When you send a frame through WebSocket over STOMP, the message will first reach `clientInboundChannel`. There, it will be routed to a specific `MessageHandler` depending on the destination name. If the name starts with /app, then it will route it to the `SimpAnnotationMethod` message handler (which will eventually call your `@MessageMapping` annotated method inside the `@Controller` class). If the name starts with /topic, then it will route it directly to the SimpleBroker[4] message handler.

Let's look at an example of the frame `SEND /app/a`. First, `clientInboundChannel` will receive and forward it to the `SimpAnnotationMethod` message handler. Then, from the `@MessageMapping` annotated method, the message will be forwarded to `brokerChannel`. This will send it to the `SimpleBroker` message handler. This message handler keeps a `ConcurrentHashMap` with every WebSocket session ID for every connected client and also all the subscriptions in the `SubscriptionRegistry` (in memory). Then, the message handler uses the WebSocket client ID to forward the message to the corresponding `clientOutboundChannel`, which will finally send the message to the client.

⚠ Note that using the simple broker approach, the subscriptions are kept in memory.

---

[4]https://github.com/spring-projects/spring-framework/blob/master/spring-messaging/src/main/java/org/springframework/messaging/simp/broker/SimpleBrokerMessageHandler.java

10.4   Message Flow Using a Full External STOMP Broker

Figure 10-2 shows the same message flow, except that here instead of keeping the in-memory subscriptions, the message handler will delegate the subscriptions to an external STOMP broker. Can you understand why this is so important? You'll learn why in the next chapter!

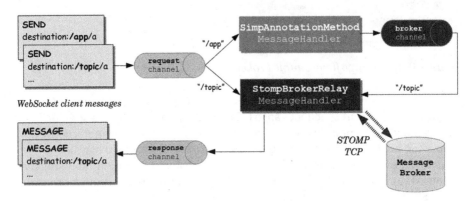

Figure 10-2. *Message flow: full external STOMP broker*

ⓘ Check out the list of STOMP brokers[5] that are available.

ⓘ In the chat app, you will use RabbitMQ with the STOMP plug-in[6] as a full external STOMP broker.

You will learn much more about Spring WebSocket in Part 3, "Code by Feature."

---

[5]https://stomp.github.io/implementations.html
[6]https://www.rabbitmq.com/web-stomp.html

CHAPTER 11

■ ■ ■

Single-Node Chat Architecture

Figure 11-1 shows the simplified architecture diagram for the single-node chat application. It shows exactly what you are running on your local machine right now if you followed the steps in Chapter 2.

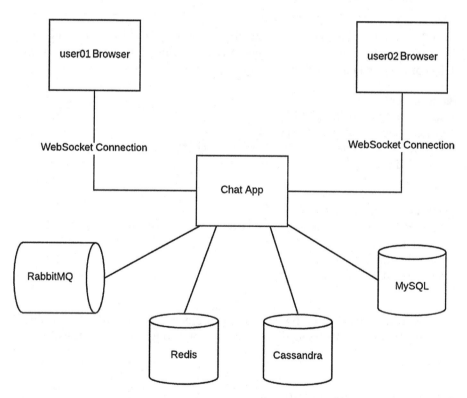

Figure 11-1. *Single-node chat application*

© Jorge Acetozi 2017
J. Acetozi, *Pro Java Clustering and Scalability*, DOI 10.1007/978-1-4842-2985-9_11

When you register a new account, the user is stored in MySQL, and the role ROLE_USER is assigned to the user, which means that this user is not allowed to create new chat rooms.

After you sign in, the list of all available chat rooms is displayed. The chat rooms and their connected users are stored in Redis as a Redis Hash[1] data type. Basically, a Redis Hash is a data structure that allows you to associate many key : value entries to a unique key. In the following example, the unique key is chatrooms:c4f045bb-8dfd-4620-b365-fd3b4fbeb46e:

```
HGETALL chatrooms:c4f045bb-8dfd-4620-b365-fd3b4fbeb46e

"id" : "c4f045bb-8dfd-4620-b365-fd3b4fbeb46e"
"name" : "Top Guitarists"
"description" : "Meet the most amazing guitarists"
```

HGETALL[2] is the Redis command that gets a hash and all the key : value entries associated with it.

When you join a chat room, a JavaScript code snippet gets executed on the client side. It starts a WebSocket over STOMP connection to the chat server. If the connection fails, it will retry every ten seconds.

```
function connect() {
  socket = new SockJS('/ws');
  stompClient = Stomp.over(socket);
  stompClient.connect({ 'chatRoomId' : chatRoomId }, stompSuccess,
  stompFailure);
}

function stompFailure(error) {
  errorMessage("Lost connection to WebSocket! Reconnecting in 10
  seconds...");
  disableInputMessage();
  setTimeout(connect, 10000);
}
```

As you've learned, after the WebSocket connection is established, everything happens through the WebSocket connection, not through HTTP requests.

---

[1]https://redis.io/topics/data-types
[2]https://redis.io/commands/hgetall

```
function stompSuccess(frame) {
  enableInputMessage();
  successMessage("Your WebSocket connection was successfully
  established!")

  stompClient.subscribe('/chatroom/connected.users',
  updateConnectedUsers);
  stompClient.subscribe('/chatroom/old.messages', oldMessages);

  stompClient.subscribe('/topic/' + chatRoomId + '.public.messages',
  publicMessages);
  stompClient.subscribe('/user/queue/' + chatRoomId + '.private.
  messages', privateMessages);
  stompClient.subscribe('/topic/' + chatRoomId + '.connected.users',
  updateConnectedUsers);
}
```

As soon as the WebSocket connection starts, these main things happen:

- The client asks for the connected users and their old messages (the entire conversation) associated with this chat room. The conversation is fetched from Cassandra.

- The client also subscribes to start receiving updates when a user joins or leaves the chat room, when a public message is sent, or when a user receives a private message.

On the server side, as soon as a user connects, the chat room is updated on Redis to add the new connected user.

In the chat room, all messages that appear to the user (public, private, and system messages) are appended to the user's conversation in Cassandra.

ⓘ System messages are those public messages sent by the admin to inform everyone that a user has joined or left the chat room.

Note that on a single-node architecture, from a functional perspective, the in-memory broker approach would work perfectly because every subscription would be kept in the server's memory, and every WebSocket connection would be bound to the same server as well.

CHAPTER 12

■ ■ ■

Multinode Chat Architecture

Imagine that you want to horizontally scale the chat application by running two instances of the chat app on different servers. Suppose you are using an in-memory SimpleBroker as well.

In Figure 12-1, Jorge and John have a WebSocket connection to server 1, and Xuxa has a WebSocket connection to server 2. What would happen if Jorge tries to send a message to Xuxa? Well, I think you already know the answer! Since Xuxa is not connected to server 1, that server doesn't know about the user Xuxa. Thus, the message will be lost. However, if Jorge sends a message to John, it will work.

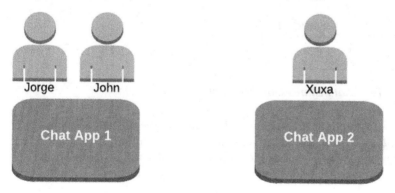

Figure 12-1. *Two chat instances: simple broker*

The in-memory approach doesn't work at all for horizontally scaling your chat application.

© Jorge Acetozi 2017

J. Acetozi, *Pro Java Clustering and Scalability*, DOI 10.1007/978-1-4842-2985-9_12

12.1 Using RabbitMQ As a Full External STOMP Broker

Now, if you start using a full external STOMP broker like RabbitMQ, you would have a scenario like the one shown in Figure 12-2.

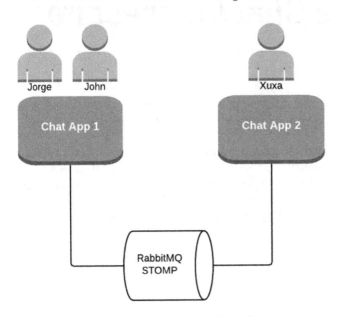

Figure 12-2. *Two chat instances: broker relay*

Now the subscriptions are not bound to specific server instances; that is, the subscriptions are not kept in the servers' memory anymore. There is an external component that's responsible for handling subscriptions. The Spring configuration for this scenario would look something like this:

```
protected void configureStompEndpoints(StompEndpointRegistry
registry) {
  registry.addEndpoint("/ws").withSockJS();
}

public void configureMessageBroker(MessageBrokerRegistry registry) {
  registry.enableStompBrokerRelay("/queue/",  "/topic/")
    .setUserDestinationBroadcast("/topic/unresolved.user.dest")
      .setUserRegistryBroadcast("/topic/registry.broadcast")
```

```
        .setRelayHost(relayHost)
        .setRelayPort(relayPort);

    registry.setApplicationDestinationPrefixes("/chatroom");
}
```

Let's take a look at these configurations:

- *enableStompBrokerRelay*: This uses an external full STOMP broker instead of an in-memory broker.

- *setRelayHost and setRelayPort*: These are the host and the port, respectively, of the external STOMP broker (RabbitMQ, in this case).

- *setUserDestinationBroadcast*: A user destination may remain unresolved because the user is connected to a different server (like Jorge and Xuxa). In such cases, this destination is used to broadcast unresolved messages so that other servers have a chance to try.

- *setUserRegistryBroadcast*: This sets a destination to broadcast the content of the local user registry (the place where connected clients are stored in memory) and to listen to such broadcasts from other servers. In a multinode architecture, this allows each server's user registry to be aware of users connected to other servers. In other words, it enables Chat App 1 to be aware that Xuxa exists in Chat App 2.

When the application starts, only the destinations /topic/unresolved. user.dest and /topic/registry.broadcast are created on RabbitMQ. Spring keeps a "system" TCP connection between the server and RabbitMQ that is not used for user messages; it's used only for internal communication between the server and the broker (such as sending heartbeat messages every ten seconds, by default, to check whether the broker is alive). If Spring detects that there is a broker outage, then it will try to reconnect every five seconds by default.

For every new WebSocket connection, the server creates a new TCP connection with the broker. This is the connection actually used for user messages.

Now that you have a solution for a multinode architecture, you could add more chat app instances behind a load balancer such as Nginx[1] and have a pretty scalable architecture, as shown in Figure 12-3.

---

[1]https://www.nginx.com/blog/websocket-nginx/

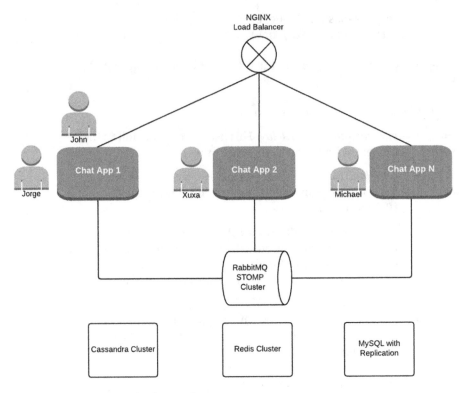

Figure 12-3. *Multinode chat architecture*

Note that every component of this architecture can be clustered and can implement a replication strategy. This means that even if some nodes experience a failure event, this architecture would keep working. This is beautiful!

There are many aspects that you should consider when dealing with scalability, for instance, increasing the number of socket descriptors that the operating system is able to use. You must keep in mind that horizontal scalability is amazing, but there are many things you can try before adding more nodes (and more costs) to your infrastructure.

CHAPTER 13

■ ■ ■

Horizontally Scaling Stateful Web Applications

Let's forget the WebSocket technology for a while and think about traditional web applications. You have already learned about the request/response HTTP model, and you know that HTTP is stateless. This means that after a server gives a response to a request, it closes the TCP connection, and it doesn't know anything about the client (not even if the client is going to make other requests) anymore. This might work in some cases, but think of an online store. How would the store be able to keep the shopping cart items across multiple requests if HTTP is stateless? To address this issue, web servers provide an HTTP session mechanism, which is basically local per-user storage that is associated with a specific code (in Java, the JSESSIONID code). When a user sends the first request to a server, it creates a new HTTP session and sends the JSESSIONID code to the user by using cookies. If the client sends a second request, the JSESSIONID code will be available in the HTTP request, and the server will be able to identify that it is a returning user. This means that if the shopping cart is stored in the HTTP session, the server will be able to keep it across requests.

This might sound nice, but it's a big issue when it comes to horizontal scalability. Can you guess why? What would happen if an online store's multinode architecture is implemented using a load balancer and a user named Jorge has his shopping cart stored in the HTTP session on server 1 and in the next request the load balancer sends it to server 2? His shopping cart wouldn't be available there, right? (See Figure 13-1.)

© Jorge Acetozi 2017

J. Acetozi, *Pro Java Clustering and Scalability*, DOI 10.1007/978-1-4842-2985-9_13

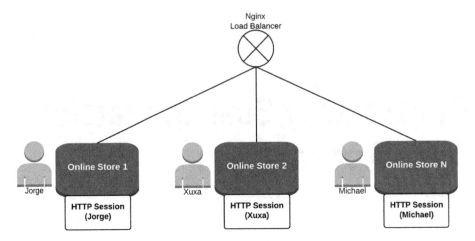

Figure 13-1. *Multinode online store without a session manager*

13.1 Using the Sticky Session Strategy

You may be thinking, "OK, but what if the load balancer always sends the requests from a specific user to a specific server? Then the user's HTTP session will always be there. Hence, the user's shopping cart will always be available across requests until this HTTP session expires." You are absolutely correct, and this is what you would call a *sticky session strategy*. But the problem arises again when you think of a node failure scenario.

Imagine that a load balancer is using the sticky session strategy and every user request is being routed to the same server. Everything is working flawlessly. But suddenly this server crashes (meaning the user's HTTP session is gone), and the load balancer is forced to forward the user to another server. What happens then? Again, the user's shopping cart is lost.

Also, what would happen if the developers deploy a new version of the online store application while the user is online? Well, there is no magic that takes place; the server will have to be restarted in order to apply the new release version, so what would happen with the user's HTTP session again? You already know the answer. But...you also already know the solution because this is similar to what you already did regarding the WebSocket technology when adding RabbitMQ as a full external STOMP broker to your architecture.

Why don't you persist the HTTP sessions in your already working relational database? Well, that's pretty much the same as the scenario used in Chapter 7 in the "Redis Overview" section. Do you remember that querying a relational database is much more expensive than querying an in-memory solution such as Redis?

Figure 13-2 shows the architecture using Redis as the session manager. Don't you think that now the architecture looks much better? If a node crashes and the load balancer redirects the user to another server instance, there is no problem. The server will notice that it doesn't have locally this specific JSESSIONID code associated with any user's HTTP session, so it will query Redis looking for it. Once it finds the user's session on Redis, it brings it back to the server's memory, and everything keeps working. The load balancer now will continue sending requests to this server because it's using a sticky session. The user doesn't even know that all these things happened behind the scenes. Good shopping, dear user!

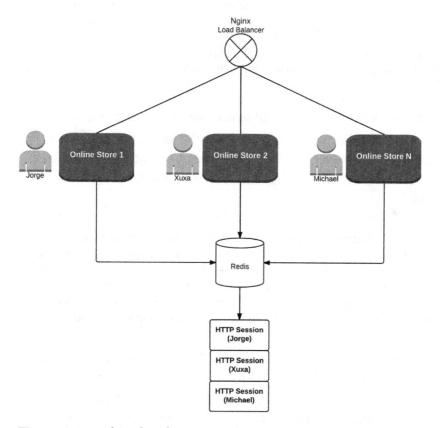

Figure 13-2. *Multinode online store with Redis as session manager*

The question now is, how would you implement this mechanism on the server side so that it fetches Redis for HTTP sessions? Well, if you use the Spring Framework, there is the amazing Spring Session[1] subproject that takes care of this for you. It's insanely easy to use Spring Session along with Redis, especially when you are setting up configurations with the help of Spring Boot.

13.2   Spring Session and WebSocket

You are using Spring Session in the chat application to store HTTP sessions on Redis, but here the scenario is a little bit different.

In Spring, when you open a new WebSocket connection, on the server side it creates a new WebSocket session. By the way, you already know that these WebSocket sessions are stored in the corresponding MessageHandler. This WebSocket session will stay alive until one of the parts explicitly closes it or the HTTP session expires. This is the way JSR-356[2] works.

Don't get confused here. The HTTP session and the WebSocket session are different things. The HTTP session is created when the user performs the first HTTP request to a server. However, the WebSocket session is created only after the user already has an HTTP session associated and successfully performs the WebSocket handshake.

The issue is that JSR-356 doesn't have a mechanism for intercepting WebSocket messages. In other words, when you are using only the WebSocket connection without performing any HTTP requests, the server assumes that the HTTP session is inactive, and as you know, every HTTP session has an expiration threshold. If this threshold is crossed, then the server will kill the user's HTTP session, and by doing this, the user's WebSocket connection will be gone as well.

To paraphrase the Spring Session documentation,[3] consider an e-mail application that does much of its work through HTTP requests. Say there is also a chat application embedded within it that works over WebSocket APIs. If a user is actively chatting with someone, you should not time out the HttpSession since that would create a pretty poor user experience. However, this is exactly what JSR-356 does.

---

[1]http://projects.spring.io/spring-session/
[2]https://jcp.org/en/jsr/detail?id=356
[3]https://github.com/spring-projects/spring-session/blob/master/docs/src/docs/asciidoc/index.adoc#websocket-why

Furthermore, according to JSR-356, if the HttpSession times out, any WebSocket that was created with that HttpSession and an authenticated user should be forcibly closed. This means that if you are actively chatting in your application and are not using the HttpSession, then you will also disconnect from your conversation.

In order to address this issue, Spring Session can be configured to ensure that WebSocket messages will keep your HttpSession alive. To configure Spring Session along with Spring WebSocket in the chat app, you need to do the following:

1. Add the Spring Session dependency in pom.xml.

```
<dependency>
  <groupId>org.springframework.session</groupId>
  <artifactId>spring-session</artifactId>
</dependency>
```

2. In application.yml, configure Spring Session with storage-type as redis as follows:

```
spring:
  session:
    store-type: redis
```

3. Now, in the WebSocket configuration class, instead of extending from AbstractWebSocketMessageBrokerConfigurer as you did in Chapter 10 in the "WebSocket over STOMP Configuration" section, you extend from AbstractSessionWebSocketMessageBrokerConfigurer<ExpiringSession>. Also, add the EnableScheduling annotation to the class declaration.

```
@Configuration
@EnableScheduling
@EnableWebSocketMessageBroker
public class WebSocketConfigSpringSession extends AbstractSessionWebSocketMessageBrokerConfigurer<ExpiringSession> {
    ...
}
```

That's it. You can pause for a coffee now, thinking about how amazing Spring is.

PART 3

■ ■ ■

Code by Feature

In this part of the book, I will discuss the code for every feature in the chat application. Again, this book is not intended to teach the fundamentals of Spring, so I'll assume you already have a basic understanding of dependency injection, controllers, services, and so on.

🔑 If you need to improve your skills with the Spring Framework, I recommend you check out the official Spring Framework documentation.[1] It offers many examples and nice tutorials as well.

---

[1] https://spring.io/docs

CHAPTER 14

■ ■ ■

Changing the Application Language

It's possible to translate all the chat application text by choosing the desired language in the application menu (Figure 14-1). This way, users from different countries can make better use of the system. This concept is frequently known as *internationalization* (or I18N).

Figure 14-1. *Language menu*

Implementing internationalization using Spring MVC[1] is quite simple.

Basically, you need the @Configuration class to extend from WebMvcConfigurerAdapter to do some Spring MVC configurations.

```
@Configuration
public class WebConfig extends WebMvcConfigurerAdapter {
  @Bean
  public LocaleResolver localeResolver() {
    return new SessionLocaleResolver();
  }
```

---

[1]https://docs.spring.io/spring/docs/current/spring-framework-reference/htmlsingle/#mvc-localeresolver

© Jorge Acetozi 2017
J. Acetozi, *Pro Java Clustering and Scalability*, DOI 10.1007/978-1-4842-2985-9_14

```
@Bean
public LocaleChangeInterceptor localeChangeInterceptor() {
  LocaleChangeInterceptor localeChangeInterceptor = new
  LocaleChangeInterceptor();
  localeChangeInterceptor.setParamName("lang");
  return localeChangeInterceptor;
}

@Override
public void addInterceptors(InterceptorRegistry registry) {
  registry.addInterceptor(localeChangeInterceptor());
  }
}
```

In this class, you set up the @Bean for the LocaleResolver. Spring has many LocaleResolver implementations such as SessionLocaleResolver and CookieLocaleResolver.

- *SessionLocaleResolver*: This will keep a locale attribute in the user's HTTP session, so as long as the user's HTTP session is active, the locale used for this user will be the one specified in the HTTP session locale attribute.

- *CookieLocaleResolver*: This uses a cookie sent back to the user. This option is particularly useful for stateless applications that don't use HTTP sessions.

In the previous configuration, LocaleChangeInterceptor will intercept each request to check whether there is a lang parameter present. Suppose that a GET request is fired with the lang=pt parameter. Basically, this interceptor would intercept this request, set the user's locale to pt (Portuguese), and store it in the user's HTTP session locale attribute. From now on, all application texts will be read from the resource bundle messages_pt.properties.

The following is the code for the menu items. When you click the English or Portuguese menu item, a GET request will be fired with the respective param attribute (en or pt).

```
<ul class="dropdown-menu">
  <li><a  id="english" href="?lang=en" th:text="#{menu.language.
  english}">English</a></li>
  <li><a id="portuguese" href="?lang=pt" th:text="#{menu.language.
  portuguese}">Portuguese</a></li>
</ul>
```

To read messages from the appropriate resource bundle (based on the locale set), Thymeleaf[2] can help you with th:text.

```
<h3 th:text="#{login.title}">Login</h3>
```

This code means that the value for the key login.title will be shown inside the h3 Hypertext Markup Language (HTML) element.

---

[2]https://www.thymeleaf.org/

CHAPTER 15

■ ■ ■

Login

Let's start understanding some Spring Security configurations.

```
@Configuration
@EnableGlobalMethodSecurity(prePostEnabled = true)
public class WebSecurityConfig extends WebSecurityConfigurerAdapter {
    @Autowired
    private UserDetailsService userDetailsService;

    @Override
    protected void configure(HttpSecurity http) throws Exception {
        http
            .csrf().disable()
            .formLogin()
                .loginProcessingUrl("/login")
                .loginPage("/")
                .defaultSuccessUrl("/chat")
                .and()
            .logout()
                .logoutSuccessUrl("/")
                .and()
            .authorizeRequests()
                .antMatchers("/login", "/new-account", "/").permitAll()
                .antMatchers(HttpMethod.POST,  "/chatroom").hasRole("ADMIN")
                .anyRequest().authenticated();
    }
```

```
@Autowired
public void configureGlobal(AuthenticationManagerBuilder auth)
throws Exception {
  auth
    .userDetailsService(userDetailsService)
    .passwordEncoder(bCryptPasswordEncoder());
}

@Bean
public BCryptPasswordEncoder bCryptPasswordEncoder() {
  return new BCryptPasswordEncoder();
}
}
```

In the configure method, everything is done using the HttpSecurity object, which provides a fluent interface.[1]

- The authentication will be done by a login web form.

- When the form submits a POST to /login, Spring Security will take care of the authentication for you.

- The login page is the root context, /.

- When the login succeeds, the user will be redirected to the /chat URI.

- The logout URI is /logout, and after the logout action, the user will be redirected to the / URI, which is the login page.

- The URIs /login, /new-account, and / are allowed for everybody (including anonymous users).

- A POST to /chatroom (to create a chat room) is allowed only by users with the role ROLE_ADMIN.

- Any other requests are allowed only by logged-in users.

When the form login is submitted to POST /login, Spring Security will intercept the request and query the MySQL instance to fetch the user and check whether the provided credentials are correct. However, if you don't instruct Spring on how to do that, things are not going to work. It's not that magical! That's why you need to implement the UserDetailsService Spring interface to instruct Spring on how to do that. Fortunately, as you learned in Chapter 8 in the "Spring Data JPA Repositories" section, you are using UserRepository, which already provides an easy way to perform User operations against the MySQL instance.

---

[1]https://www.martinfowler.com/bliki/FluentInterface.html

```
@Service
public class UserDetailsServiceImpl implements UserDetailsService {

    @Autowired
    private UserRepository userRepository;

    @Override
    public UserDetails loadUserByUsername(String username) throws
    UsernameNotFoundException {
        User user = userRepository.findOne(username);

        if (user == null) {
            throw new UsernameNotFoundException("User not found");
        } else {
            Set<SimpleGrantedAuthority> grantedAuthorities
            = user.getRoles().stream().map(role -> new
            SimpleGrantedAuthority(role.getName())).collect
            (Collectors.toSet());

            return new org.springframework.security.core.
            userdetails.User(user.getUsername(), user.getPassword(),
            grantedAuthorities);
        }
    }
}
```

In the previous code snippet, UserRepository is used to query the database looking for the given username. Note that an instance of the UserDetailsService is provided to AuthenticationManagerBuilder in the configuration class.

The BCryptPasswordEncoder component is used to encrypt the user's password using bcrypt.[2]

ℹ Here, we are disabling cross-site request forgery (CSRF) protection[3] to simplify things. If you want to enable it, just remove the .csrf().disable() line and add <input type="hidden" th:name="${_csrf.parameterName}" th:value="${_csrf. token}"/> to the HTML forms to send the CSRF token with the form data. Also, if you enable it, the /logout will need to be a POST request.

---

[2]https://en.wikipedia.org/wiki/Bcrypt
[3]https://docs.spring.io/spring-security/site/docs/current/reference/
html/csrf.html

New Account

The following code is the User class. Along with the attributes declaration, you use the Bean Validation[1] and Hibernate Validator[2] annotations. A valid new user must have the following:

- username: This must not be empty and must have between 5 and 15 characters. This field is the user database table's primary key.

- password: This must not be empty and must have a minimum of five characters.

- name: This must not be empty.

- email: This must not be empty and must be a valid e-mail address.

```
@Entity
@Table(name = "user")
public class User {
  @Id
  @NotEmpty
  @Size(min = 5, max = 15)
  private String username;

  @NotEmpty
  @Size(min = 5)
  private String password;
```

---

[1]http://beanvalidation.org/1.1/spec/
[2]http://hibernate.org/validator/

```
@NotEmpty
private String name;

@Email
@NotEmpty
private String email;

@ManyToMany(fetch=FetchType.EAGER)
@JoinTable(name = "user_role",
           joinColumns = @JoinColumn(name = "username"),
           inverseJoinColumns = @JoinColumn(name = "role_id"))
private Set<Role> roles = new HashSet<>();
...
}
```

In addition to these simple validations, you must be sure that the provided username doesn't exist. For this, you create a custom Spring validator.

```
@Component
public class NewUserValidator implements Validator {
  @Autowired
  private UserRepository userRepository;

  @Override
  public boolean supports(Class<?> clazz) {
    return User.class.isAssignableFrom(clazz);
  }

  @Override
  public void validate(Object target, Errors errors) {
    User newUser = (User) target;
    if (userRepository.exists(newUser.getUsername())) {
      errors.rejectValue("username", "new.account.username.already.
      exists");
    }
  }
}
```

Basically, NewUserValidator implements the Validator Spring interface and uses UserRepository to query the database to check whether the username already exists. If it exists, then a new error is added to the Errors object.

ℹ️ Note that the added error contains the key of the error message, which is
`new.account.username.already.exists`. You can check its value in the appendix.

Once the form in `new-account.html` is submitted, the `createAccount` method is called in `AuthenticationController`.

```
@Controller
public class AuthenticationController {
  @Autowired
  private UserService userService;

  @Autowired
  private NewUserValidator newUserValidator;

  @InitBinder
  protected void initBinder(WebDataBinder binder) {
   binder.addValidators(newUserValidator);
  }

  @RequestMapping(path = "/new-account", method = RequestMethod.
  POST)
  public String createAccount(@Valid User user, BindingResult
  bindingResult) {
    if (bindingResult.hasErrors()) {
      return "new-account";
    }
    userService.createUser(user);
    return "redirect:/";
  }
}
```

Note that you added `NewUserValidator` to the validators. This makes Spring use your custom validator as well as the simple validations in the `User` class against the new `User` object annotated with `@Valid`. If there are any errors, the user is redirected to the new account form and the errors are shown, as in Figure 16-1.

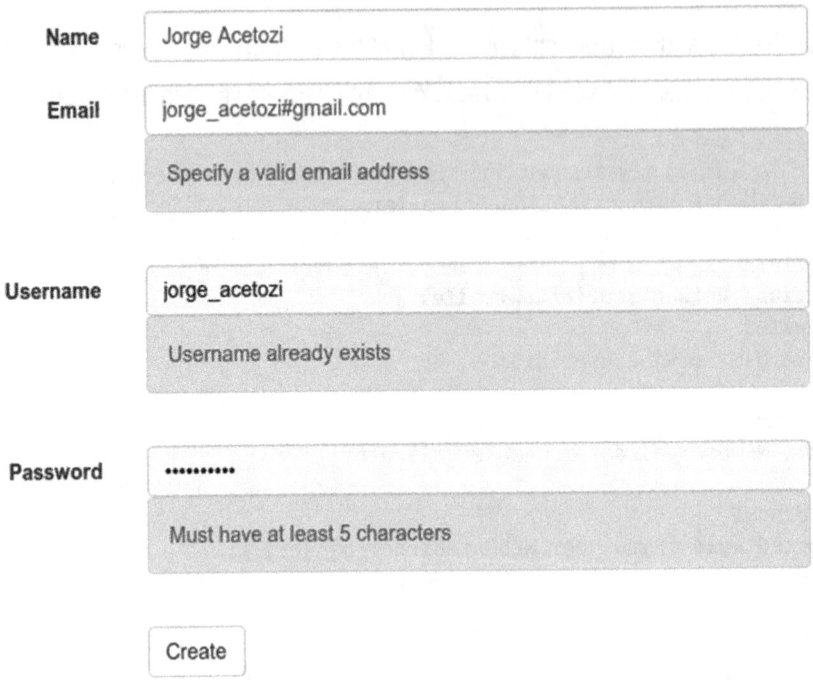

Name	Jorge Acetozi

Email	jorge_acetozi#gmail.com
	Specify a valid email address

Username	jorge_acetozi
	Username already exists

Password	••••••••••
	Must have at least 5 characters

Create

Figure 16-1. *Validations*

To automatically display the error messages in the page, Thymeleaf provides
th:errors.

```
<div class="form-group">
    <label for="username"
            th:text="#{new.account.username}">
            Username
    </label>
    <div>
        <input th:field="${user.username}"
                type="text"
                id="username"
                name="username"
                th:placeholder="#{new.account.your.username}" />
        <div th:errors="*{username}">Error</div>
    </div>
</div>
```

When everything is correct with the submitted user, then `userService.createUser(user)` is called.

```
@Service
public class DefaultUserService implements UserService {
  @Autowired
  private UserRepository userRepository;

  @Autowired
  private RoleRepository roleRepository;

  @Autowired
  private BCryptPasswordEncoder bCryptPasswordEncoder;

  @Override
  @Transactional
  public User createUser(User user) {
    user.setPassword(bCryptPasswordEncoder.encode(user.
    getPassword()));
    Role userRole = roleRepository.findByName("ROLE_USER");
    user.addRoles(Arrays.asList(userRole));
    return userRepository.save(user);
  }
}
```

Essentially, this method encrypts the user's password using the BCryptPasswordEncoder component, attaches the ROLE_USER role to its roles, and saves the user into the database. As ROLE_USER does not allow you to create new chat rooms, every new user will not be able to use this feature.

CHAPTER 17

▨ ▨ ▨

New Chat Room

In this chapter, I illustrate how easy it is to work with REST endpoints in Spring MVC.

On the client side, you just create a JavaScript object called newChatRoom, convert it to JSON format, and send a POST request to the /chatroom endpoint. If it succeeds, then the success callback is called, and it appends the new chat room to the grid by manipulating the Document Object Model[1] (DOM).

```
function createNewChatRoom() {
  var newChatRoom = {
    'name' : txtNewChatRoomName.val(),
    'description' : txtNewChatRoomDescription.val()
  };

  $.ajax({
    type : "POST",
    url : "/chatroom",
    data : JSON.stringify(newChatRoom),
    contentType : "application/json",
    success : function(chatRoom) {
        //append chat room to the grid
    },
  });
}
```

---

[1]https://www.w3schools.com/js/js_htmldom.asp

17.1   Secured REST Endpoints with Spring MVC and Spring Security

Spring MVC will first convert the JSON in the HTTP request body (that's why you use the @RequestBody annotation) to the chatroom object and call the createChatRoom method. This method will use the chatRoomService component to save the chatroom object in Redis. After that, the createChatRoom method will convert the new chatroom object into a JSON representation and append it to the HTTP response body (that's why you used the @ResponseBody annotation) along with an HTTP 201 CREATED status code.

⚠ Note that by using the @Secured("ROLE_ADMIN") annotation, you tell Spring Security to allow only logged-in users with the role ROLE_ADMIN to consume this endpoint. Otherwise, it will automatically send a 403 FORBIDDEN status code to the client.

```
@Controller
public class ChatRoomController {
  @Autowired
  private ChatRoomService chatRoomService;

  @Secured("ROLE_ADMIN")
  @RequestMapping(path = "/chatroom", method = RequestMethod.POST)
  @ResponseBody
  @ResponseStatus(code = HttpStatus.CREATED)
  public ChatRoom createChatRoom(@RequestBody ChatRoom chatRoom) {
    return chatRoomService.save(chatRoom);
  }
}

@Service
public class RedisChatRoomService implements ChatRoomService {
  @Autowired
  private ChatRoomRepository chatRoomRepository;

  @Override
  public ChatRoom save(ChatRoom chatRoom) {
    return chatRoomRepository.save(chatRoom);
  }
}
```

■ ■ ■

CHAPTER 18

Joining the Chat Room

When you join a chat room, some JavaScript code gets executed on the client side.

```javascript
function connect() {
  socket = new SockJS('/ws');
  stompClient = Stomp.over(socket);
  stompClient.connect({ 'chatRoomId' : chatRoomId }, stompSuccess,
  stompFailure);
}

function stompSuccess(frame) {
  enableInputMessage();
  successMessage("Your WebSocket connection was successfully
  established!")

  stompClient.subscribe('/chatroom/connected.users',
  updateConnectedUsers);
  stompClient.subscribe('/chatroom/old.messages',  oldMessages);

  stompClient.subscribe('/topic/' + chatRoomId + '.public.messages',
  publicMessages);
  stompClient.subscribe('/user/queue/' + chatRoomId + '.private.
  messages', privateMessages);
  stompClient.subscribe('/topic/' + chatRoomId + '.connected.users',
  updateConnectedUsers);
}

function stompFailure(error) {
  errorMessage("Lost connection to WebSocket! Reconnecting in
  10 seconds...");
  disableInputMessage();
  setTimeout(connect, 10000);
}
```

© Jorge Acetozi 2017
J. Acetozi, *Pro Java Clustering and Scalability*, DOI 10.1007/978-1-4842-2985-9_18

First, the connect function is called, and a new WebSocket connection is started using STOMP as a subprotocol. Note that you also add the header 'chatRoomId' : chatRoomId when you send the CONNECT frame because the server must keep this information to ensure that it's manipulating the correct destination names.

If the handshake succeeds, then the stompSuccess function is called, and the user subscribes to some destinations. Actually, the first two subscriptions are executed only once on the server side, and they are used to get some initial data, that is, his old conversation and the current connected users to this specific chat room. This is the Java code executed when these two subscriptions happen:

```java
@Controller
public class ChatRoomController {
  @Autowired
  private ChatRoomService chatRoomService;

  @Autowired
  private InstantMessageService instantMessageService;

  @SubscribeMapping("/connected.users")
  public List<ChatRoomUser> listChatRoomConnectedUsersOnSubscribe
  (SimpMessageHeaderAccessor headerAccessor) {
    String chatRoomId = headerAccessor.getSessionAttributes().get
    ("chatRoomId").toString();
    return chatRoomService.findById(chatRoomId).getConnectedUsers();
  }

  @SubscribeMapping("/old.messages")
  public List<InstantMessage> listOldMessagesFromUserOnSubscribe
  (Principal principal, SimpMessageHeaderAccessor headerAccessor) {
    String chatRoomId = headerAccessor.getSessionAttributes().get
    ("chatRoomId").toString();
    return instantMessageService.findAllInstantMessagesFor
    (principal.getName(), chatRoomId);
  }
  ...
}
```

ℹ️ The `List<ChatRoomUser>` list is fetched from Redis, and the `List<InstantMessage>` list is fetched from Cassandra.

ℹ️ The `@SubscribeMapping` annotation is useful when users need to fetch the initial data using the WebSocket connection.

The last three subscriptions in the JavaScript code are the following, respectively:

- Execute the `publicMessages` function when a new message arrives at the `'/topic/' + chatRoomId + '.public.messages'` destination. This function will render a public message in the user's message panel.

- Execute the `privateMessages` function when a new message arrives at the `'/user/queue/' + chatRoomId + '.private.messages'` destination. This function will render a private message in the user's message panel.

- Execute the `updateConnectedUsers` function when a new message arrives at the `'/topic/' + chatRoomId + '.connected.users'` destination. This function will update the connected users in the user's connected users panel.

18.1 WebSocket Reconnection Strategy

When the WebSocket connection is lost, the `stompFailure` function is executed, and it will try to reestablish the connection every ten seconds. If it succeeds, then everything explained earlier happens again. Because every message is stored in Cassandra (regardless of being delivered through the WebSocket connection), even if the user was offline while someone sent a message to him, when the user reconnects, the message will be in the `List<InstantMessage>` list and will be displayed in the user's message panel.

18.2 WebSocket Events

Once the WebSocket connection is established or disconnected, an event is triggered on the server side, and a system message is sent to every connected user in the chat room informing them that someone has joined or left (Figure 18-1).

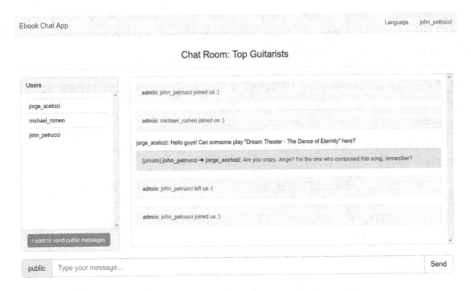

Figure 18-1. *System messages from admin*

The following is the code that handles these events on the server side:

```
@Component
public class WebSocketEvents {
  @Autowired
  private ChatRoomService chatRoomService;

  @EventListener
  private void handleSessionConnected(SessionConnectEvent event) {
    SimpMessageHeaderAccessor headers = SimpMessageHeaderAccessor.
    wrap(event.getMessage());
    String chatRoomId = headers.getNativeHeader("chatRoomId").
    get(0);
    headers.getSessionAttributes().put("chatRoomId", chatRoomId);
    ChatRoomUser joiningUser = new ChatRoomUser(event.getUser().
    getName());

    chatRoomService.join(joiningUser, chatRoomService.
    findById(chatRoomId));
  }
```

```
@EventListener
private void handleSessionDisconnect(SessionDisconnectEvent event) {
  SimpMessageHeaderAccessor headers = SimpMessageHeaderAccessor.
  wrap(event.getMessage());
  String chatRoomId = headers.getSessionAttributes().
  get("chatRoomId").toString();
  ChatRoomUser leavingUser = new ChatRoomUser(event.getUser().
  getName());

  chatRoomService.leave(leavingUser, chatRoomService.
  findById(chatRoomId));
  }
}
```

Let's take the SessionConnected event as an example and follow the entire flow.

The handleSessionConnected method is called when a WebSocket connection is created. Then, the chatRoomId value is obtained from the CONNECT frame headers, and it's stored in the user's WebSocket session as an attribute. This is convenient since from now every message the client sends doesn't need to provide the chatRoomId value, as it's already stored in the user's WebSocket session. Then, the join method is called, passing joiningUser and chatRoom as parameters.

```
@Service
public class RedisChatRoomService implements ChatRoomService {
  @Autowired
  private SimpMessagingTemplate webSocketMessagingTemplate;

  @Autowired
  private ChatRoomRepository chatRoomRepository;

  @Autowired
  private InstantMessageService instantMessageService;

  @Override
  public ChatRoom join(ChatRoomUser joiningUser, ChatRoom chatRoom) {
    chatRoom.addUser(joiningUser);
    chatRoomRepository.save(chatRoom);

    sendPublicMessage(SystemMessages.welcome(chatRoom.getId(),
    joiningUser.getUsername()));
    updateConnectedUsersViaWebSocket(chatRoom);
    return chatRoom;
  }
```

```java
@Override
public ChatRoom leave(ChatRoomUser leavingUser, ChatRoom chatRoom) {
    sendPublicMessage(SystemMessages.goodbye(chatRoom.getId(),
    leavingUser.getUsername()));

    chatRoom.removeUser(leavingUser);
    chatRoomRepository.save(chatRoom);

    updateConnectedUsersViaWebSocket(chatRoom);
    return chatRoom;
}

@Override
public void sendPublicMessage(InstantMessage instantMessage) {
    webSocketMessagingTemplate.convertAndSend(
        Destinations.ChatRoom.publicMessages(instantMessage.
        getChatRoomId()), instantMessage);

    instantMessageService.appendInstantMessageToConversations
    (instantMessage);
}

private void updateConnectedUsersViaWebSocket(ChatRoom chatRoom) {
    webSocketMessagingTemplate.convertAndSend(
        Destinations.ChatRoom.connectedUsers(chatRoom.getId()),
        chatRoom.getConnectedUsers());
}
}
```

18.2.1   Send Public System Messages over WebSocket

Let's examine the join method now. First it adds the user to the chatRoom object and persists it in Redis; then it calls the sendPublicMessage method that uses SimpMessagingTemplate (that you've already used before in this book) and sends a public welcome message as the admin user. Every connected user is able to receive this message because it's sent to the '/topic/' + chatRoomId + '.public.messages' destination, which is one of the subscriptions that happens when a user establishes the WebSocket connection. Then, it calls the appendInstantMessageToConversations method in the InstantMessageService component, which is responsible for storing the message to the users' conversations in Cassandra. Here is the code for this method:

```java
@Service
public class CassandraInstantMessageService implements
InstantMessageService {

    @Autowired
    private InstantMessageRepository instantMessageRepository;

    @Autowired
    private ChatRoomService chatRoomService;

    @Override
    public void appendInstantMessageToConversations(InstantMessage
    instantMessage) {
      if (instantMessage.isFromAdmin() || instantMessage.isPublic()) {
        ChatRoom chatRoom = chatRoomService.findById(instantMessage.
        getChatRoomId());

        chatRoom.getConnectedUsers().forEach(connectedUser -> {
          instantMessage.setUsername(connectedUser.getUsername());
          instantMessageRepository.save(instantMessage);
        });
      } else {
        instantMessage.setUsername(instantMessage.getFromUser());
        instantMessageRepository.save(instantMessage);

        instantMessage.setUsername(instantMessage.getToUser());
        instantMessageRepository.save(instantMessage);
      }
    }

    @Override
    public List<InstantMessage> findAllInstantMessagesFor(String
    username, String chatRoomId) {
      return instantMessageRepository.findInstantMessagesByUsernameAnd
      ChatRoomId(username, chatRoomId);
    }
}
```

This code essentially saves in Cassandra the message for the involved users. For example, if you send a private message to me, this method will append the message to my conversation and to yours. But if you send a public message, then this method will append the message to each connected user's conversation.

Finally, it calls the updateConnectedUsersViaWebSocket method, which also sends a public message to the '/topic/' + chatRoomId + '.connected.users' destination. As all users have a subscription to this destination, they are able to receive the message and update their connected users panel.

Essentially, the same flow occurs when a user leaves the chat room.

■ ■ ■

CHAPTER 19

Sending a User's Public Messages over WebSocket

When the client sends a public message in the chat room, the sendMessage JavaScript function is called. Essentially, it converts the instantMessage JavaScript object into a JSON representation and sends the message to the application destination /chatroom/send.message.

```javascript
function sendMessage() {
  var instantMessage;

  if (spanSendTo.text() == "public") {
    instantMessage = {
      'text' : inputMessage.val()
    }
  } else {
    instantMessage = {
      'text' : inputMessage.val(),
      'toUser' : spanSendTo.text()
    }
  }
  stompClient.send("/chatroom/send.message", {}, JSON.stringify
  (instantMessage));
  inputMessage.val("").focus();
}
```

ℹ Refer to the "Message Flow Using a Simple Broker" section in Chapter 10 for details of how the messages are routed based on destination names.

© Jorge Acetozi 2017
J. Acetozi, *Pro Java Clustering and Scalability*, DOI 10.1007/978-1-4842-2985-9_19

In the ChatRoomController Java class, the method sendMessage is called, and the instantMessage object has the fromUser and chatRoomId fields set. Then, the chatRoomService object is called to send a private or public message. In this case, the instantMessage.isPublic() method will return true, so a public message will be sent.

```
@Controller
public class ChatRoomController {
  @Autowired
  private ChatRoomService chatRoomService;

  @MessageMapping("/send.message")
  public void sendMessage(@Payload InstantMessage instantMessage,
  Principal principal, SimpMessageHeaderAccessor headerAccessor) {
    String chatRoomId = headerAccessor.getSessionAttributes().
    get("chatRoomId").toString();
    instantMessage.setFromUser(principal.getName());
    instantMessage.setChatRoomId(chatRoomId);

    if (instantMessage.isPublic()) {
      chatRoomService.sendPublicMessage(instantMessage);
    } else {
      chatRoomService.sendPrivateMessage(instantMessage);
    }
  }
}
```

The sendPublicMessage method in the ChatRoomService class was already explained in the "Send Public System Messages over WebSocket" section of Chapter 18.

CHAPTER 20

Sending a User's Private Messages over WebSocket

Sending private messages can be a little bit trickier than sending public ones. Let's take a look at the JavaScript code, shown here:

```javascript
function sendMessage() {
  var instantMessage;

  if (spanSendTo.text() == "public") {
    instantMessage = {
      'text' : inputMessage.val()
    }
  } else {
    instantMessage = {
      'text' : inputMessage.val(),
      'toUser' : spanSendTo.text()
    }
  }
  stompClient.send("/chatroom/send.message", {}, JSON.stringify
  (instantMessage));
  inputMessage.val("").focus();
}
```

When the client sends a private message in the chat room, the sendMessage JavaScript function is called. Essentially, it converts the instantMessage JavaScript object into a JSON representation and sends the message to the application destination /chatroom/send.message, which is the same destination used for sending a user's public messages.

© Jorge Acetozi 2017
J. Acetozi, *Pro Java Clustering and Scalability*, DOI 10.1007/978-1-4842-2985-9_20

```java
@Controller
public class ChatRoomController {
  @Autowired
  private ChatRoomService chatRoomService;

  @MessageMapping("/send.message")
  public void sendMessage(@Payload InstantMessage instantMessage,
  Principal principal, SimpMessageHeaderAccessor headerAccessor) {
    String chatRoomId = headerAccessor.getSessionAttributes().
    get("chatRoomId").toString();
    instantMessage.setFromUser(principal.getName());
    instantMessage.setChatRoomId(chatRoomId);

    if (instantMessage.isPublic()) {
      chatRoomService.sendPublicMessage(instantMessage);
    } else {
      chatRoomService.sendPrivateMessage(instantMessage);
    }
  }
}
```

In the ChatRoomController Java class, the method sendMessage is called, and the instantMessage object has the fromUser and chatRoomId fields set. Then, the chatRoomService is called to send a private or a public message. In this case, the instantMessage.isPublic() method returns false, so a private message will be sent.

```java
@Service
public class RedisChatRoomService implements ChatRoomService {
  @Autowired
  private SimpMessagingTemplate webSocketMessagingTemplate;

  @Autowired
  private InstantMessageService instantMessageService;

  @Override
  public void sendPrivateMessage(InstantMessage instantMessage) {
    webSocketMessagingTemplate.convertAndSendToUser(
        instantMessage.getToUser(),
        Destinations.ChatRoom.privateMessages(instantMessage.
        getChatRoomId()), instantMessage);
```

```
    webSocketMessagingTemplate.convertAndSendToUser(
        instantMessage.getFromUser(),
        Destinations.ChatRoom.privateMessages(instantMessage.
        getChatRoomId()), instantMessage);

    instantMessageService.appendInstantMessageToConversations
    (instantMessage);
  }
}
```

If you look closely at Destinations.ChatRoom.privateMessages (instantMessage.getChatRoomId()), you will see that this static method will return a String that represents the user's private messages destination. For example, for a chat room with an ID of AG1XX5, it would be something like / queue/AG1XX5.private.messages.

When the convertAndSendToUser method is invoked, it receives the target username (the user's username that will receive the private message), the destination, and the instantMessage itself. The question now is, how can Spring can send a message to a specific user if the destination /queue/AG1XX5.private. messages says nothing about the target user? In fact, every different user who sends a private message will have this same destination name, right?

Well, Spring is smart, and behind the scenes UserDestinationMessageHandler will append to this destination the target user's WebSocket session ID. Then, if the WebSocket session ID for the target user is user123, the destination will be transformed into /queue/AG1XX5. private.messages-user123, and the message will be sent to it.

Now, for the user to receive this private message, the user must be subscribed to this destination. Let's check the JavaScript subscriptions code and find out whether the user is subscribed to the /queue/AG1XX5.private. messages-user123 destination.

```
function connect() {
  socket = new SockJS('/ws');
  stompClient = Stomp.over(socket);
  stompClient.connect({ 'chatRoomId' : chatRoomId }, stompSuccess,
  stompFailure);
}

function stompSuccess(frame) {
  ...
  stompClient.subscribe('/user/queue/' + chatRoomId + '.private.
  messages', privateMessages);
  ...
}
```

No! There is no subscription to this destination. That's weird! Well, actually when Spring detects a subscription with the prefix /user/, UserDestinationMessageHandler will again append the WebSocket session ID to the destination name and remove /user from it. So, in the end, the user will be subscribing to the /queue/AG1XX5.private.messages-user123 destination instead of /user/queue/AG1XX5.private.messages.

Well, if the user is subscribed to this destination, then he will be able to receive the private message. *Voilà!*

The question now is, why does Spring perform this magic for you? Well, if you want to send a private message to a user, you must know exactly which destination name the user is subscribed to, right? In addition, the destination name must be unique, so to get this guarantee, the WebSocket session ID is used. Is it convenient to have to know the user's WebSocket session ID in order to send a private message to him? I think you will agree with me...no! That's why Spring does this "translation" for you. It's able to retrieve the WebSocket session ID from the user's username. This allows you to send a private message to a specific user from any part of the system just by making a call like this:

```
simpMessagingTemplate.convertAndSendToUser(
    "target_username_here",
    "/queue/AG1XX5.private.messages"),
    instantMessage);
```

PART 4

■ ■ ■

Testing the Code

In this part of the book, you will learn about the importance of testing your applications and how crucial it is for implementing continuous delivery. In addition, I will discuss the test code for unit and integration tests.

ℹ This book is not intended to teach the basics of JUnit or define mocks, stubs, and so on. Instead, I'll discuss the test code written in the chat application (as I did in Part 3, "Code by Feature").

ℹ I'll show only a few examples of unit and integration tests. Please clone the GitHub chat app repository[1] to read and run all the implemented tests.

---

[1]https://github.com/jorgeacetozi/ebook-chat-app-spring-websocket-cassandra-redis-rabbitmq

CHAPTER 21

Lazy Deployments vs. Fast Deployments

Perhaps you've worked for a company where the deployment process to the production environment was very *lazy*. That is, it took many days or sometimes even months to happen. Believe it or not, in practice it's not that difficult to find these scenarios.

In short, this kind of problem is often the root cause of a software project failure. That's because taking such a long period of time to deploy a new release to production has many disadvantages.

- Clients will not be happy with features that would add value to their business being on the developers' machines instead of in production.

- The new version will have a lot of new code because developers were working on new features for a long period of time, probably introducing many bugs to the application at once. This makes it even harder to fix them (and other) bugs.

- The team will not be able to fix critical bugs and deliver the software because of the amount of time taken between deployments.

- Developers will work hard and will not see their code in production. This is really discouraging.

As you can see, there are quite a lot of reasons not to have a lazy deployment process.

J. Acetozi, *Pro Java Clustering and Scalability*, DOI 10.1007/978-1-4842-2985-9_21

ℹ I recommend the book *Continuous Delivery* from Jez Humble and David Farley (Addison-Wesley, 2010) for an excellent introduction to the amazing world of continuous delivery.

By contrast, the ability to deliver code to production in a matter of hours or even minutes brings a lot of benefits, including the following:

- You will have happy clients using new features every week, perhaps every day, and increasing value to their business.

- You get low-risk releases. Each new release includes only a small feature. If something goes wrong, it's much easier to find and fix it. This obviously implies lower costs as well.

- Bug fixes are delivered very quickly.

- Happy developers see their jobs adding value to other people.

As you can see, there are many good reasons to release new versions to production as soon as possible.

CHAPTER 22

Continuous Delivery

Continuous delivery is the ability to deliver changes (such as new features, configuration changes, bug fixes, and so on) into production safely and quickly in a sustainable way.

Of course, achieving this comes at a price. The entire delivery process (from development to production) must be highly automated. Remember, humans are good at creative tasks but horrible at repetitive tasks. Machines are horrible at creative tasks but excellent at repetitive tasks. Why not take advantage of both humans and machines? In other words, let humans and machines do what they do best!

Testing is a repetitive, difficult, and boring task. Humans are not able to test thousands of use cases without making mistakes. Machines are. Also, machines can accomplish a testing task in seconds or minutes, while humans can spend entire days doing it. This also means that replacing humans with machines on these kinds of tasks is cheaper.

Having humans testing your software or manually involved in any task that could have been automated is something that just doesn't fit in with the continuous delivery of software to production. *If you want to implement continuous delivery, automation is key!*

Can you see now why automated tests are so important? I would say that they're a sort of prerequisite for implementing continuous delivery with high-quality releases. Implementing continuous delivery without good automated tests will result in delivering terrible-quality code to production quickly. Is that what you want? Definitely, no!

J. Acetozi, *Pro Java Clustering and Scalability*, DOI 10.1007/978-1-4842-2985-9_22

CHAPTER 23

Types of Automated Tests

There are lots of types of automated tests that can be coded. All of them have their strengths and weaknesses. The following are the most common ones:

- *Unit tests*: These provide fast feedback, but they test only an isolated unit of code (say, a method in a class). For example, an issue with a SQL query would not be caught since a unit test would not hit the database. Unit tests usually are executed in seconds or even milliseconds.

- *Integration tests*: These provide slower feedback, but they include testing the external integrations such as databases or web services. That is, they are more comprehensive than unit tests. (This doesn't mean they are better! Be careful here; remember that every type of test has its own strengths and weaknesses.) Usually, integration tests are executed in minutes, but the time may vary a lot depending on the number of tests to be run.

- *Acceptance tests*: These provide even slower feedback than integration tests, but they actually simulate a user in the system using the browser and clicking buttons and links, filling in and submitting forms, and so on. Usually they are executed in minutes, but the time may vary a lot depending on the number of tests to be run.

- *Stress tests*: These consist of flooding the system with lots of requests to get feedback on how it behaves under these conditions.

Usually, unit and integration tests are most often used. Together, they cover a lot of scenarios and avoid many application issues. Also, they are easier to code than the other types of tests (considering that stress tests should run in a similar production environment, etc.).

© Jorge Acetozi 2017
J. Acetozi, *Pro Java Clustering and Scalability*, DOI 10.1007/978-1-4842-2985-9_23

ⓘ Actually, there are even more types of automated tests, such as security tests, that could be added to your application's automated test suite. The Open Web Application Security Project[1] (OWASP) is an online community that creates freely available articles, methodologies, documentation, tools, and technologies in the field of web application security. For example, the OWASP Zed Attack Proxy[2] (ZAP) is one of the world's most popular free security tools and is actively maintained by hundreds of international volunteers. This tool can help you automatically find security vulnerabilities in your web applications and can be easily integrated into your continuous delivery pipeline (it even has a Jenkins plug-in[3] available).

---

[1]https://www.owasp.org/index.php/Main_Page
[2]https://github.com/zaproxy/zaproxy
[3]https://wiki.jenkins.io/display/JENKINS/zap+plugin

CHAPTER 24

Unit Tests

Unit tests provide fast feedback, but they test only an isolated unit of code (a method in a class, for example). In the chat application, I write unit tests using JUnit[1] along with Mockito[2] and Hamcrest.[3]

24.1 InstantMessageBuilderTest.java

The InstantMessageBuilderTest.java class tests the InstantMessageBuilder class, which implements a builder pattern[4] to provide a chain of methods responsible for simplifying the creation of a new InstantMessage object.

```java
public class InstantMessageBuilderTest {
  private final String chatRoomId = "123";
  private final String fromUser = "jorge_acetozi";
  private final String toUser = "michael_romeo";
  private final String publicMessageText = "Hello guys... I hope you
  are enjoying my eBook!";
  private final String privateMessageText = "I'm listening to
  Symphony X right now!";
  private final String systemMessageText = "This is a system message
  from admin user!";
```

[1]http://junit.org/junit4/
[2]http://site.mockito.org/
[3]http://hamcrest.org/
[4]https://en.wikipedia.org/wiki/Builder_pattern

```
@Test
public void shouldCreatePublicInstantMessage() {
  InstantMessage publicMessage = new InstantMessageBuilder()
              .newMessage()
              .withChatRoomId(chatRoomId)
              .publicMessage()
              .fromUser(fromUser)
              .withText(publicMessageText);

  assertThat(publicMessage.isPublic(), is(true));
  assertThat(publicMessage.isFromAdmin(), is(false));
  assertThat(publicMessage.getChatRoomId(), is(chatRoomId));
  assertThat(publicMessage.getFromUser(), is(fromUser));
  assertThat(publicMessage.getToUser(), is(nullValue()));
  assertThat(publicMessage.getText(), is(publicMessageText));
}

@Test
public void shouldCreatePrivateInstantMessage() {
  InstantMessage privateMessage = new InstantMessageBuilder()
              .newMessage()
              .withChatRoomId(chatRoomId)
              .privateMessage()
              .toUser(toUser)
              .fromUser(fromUser).
              withText(privateMessageText);

  assertThat(privateMessage.isPublic(), is(false));
  assertThat(privateMessage.isFromAdmin(), is(false));
  assertThat(privateMessage.getChatRoomId(), is(chatRoomId));
  assertThat(privateMessage.getFromUser(), is(fromUser));
  assertThat(privateMessage.getToUser(), is(toUser));
  assertThat(privateMessage.getText(), is(privateMessageText));
}

@Test
public void shouldCreateSystemInstantMessage() {
  InstantMessage systemMessage = new InstantMessageBuilder()
              .newMessage()
              .withChatRoomId(chatRoomId)
              .systemMessage()
              .withText(systemMessageText);
```

```
    assertThat(systemMessage.isPublic(), is(true));
    assertThat(systemMessage.isFromAdmin(), is(true));
    assertThat(systemMessage.getChatRoomId(), is(chatRoomId));
    assertThat(systemMessage.getFromUser(), is(SystemUsers.ADMIN.
    getUsername()));
    assertThat(systemMessage.getToUser(), is(nullValue()));
    assertThat(systemMessage.getText(), is(systemMessageText));
  }
}
```

The tests become really easy to read when you use Hamcrest matchers. For example, in shouldCreatePublicInstantMessage, you use InstantMessageBuilder to build a public message. A message is considered to be public when the toUser field is null. However, in shouldCreatePrivateInstantMessage, the toUser field cannot be null.

In shouldCreateSystemInstantMessage, you check that every system message is public and is from a user whose username is *admin*.

24.2 DestinationsTest.java

The DestinationsTest.java class tests the Destinations class, which provides some static methods that return the destination names for subscribing to public messages, private messages, or connected users in a chat room. These tests are important because if someone changes the Destination class (even accidentally), all the chat room features will stop working.

```
public class DestinationsTest {
  private final String chatRoomId = "123";

  @Test
  public void shouldGetPublicMessagesDestination() {
    assertThat(Destinations.ChatRoom.publicMessages("123"),
    is("/topic/" + chatRoomId + ".public.messages"));
  }

  @Test
  public void shouldGetPrivateMessagesDestination() {
    assertThat(Destinations.ChatRoom.privateMessages("123"),
    is("/queue/" + chatRoomId + ".private.messages"));
  }
```

```
@Test
public void shouldGetConnectedUsersDestination() {
  assertThat(Destinations.ChatRoom.connectedUsers("123"),
  is("/topic/" + chatRoomId + ".connected.users"));
}
}
```

Basically, this class tests only if the destination names are /topic/123.
public.messages, /queue/123.private.messages, and /topic/123.
connected.users, respectively, for a given chat room ID equal to 123.

24.3   RedisChatRoomServiceTest.java

The RedisChatRoomServiceTest.java class tests the RedisChatRoomService
class, which provides methods for chat room operations.

```
@RunWith(MockitoJUnitRunner.class)
public class RedisChatRoomServiceTest {
  @InjectMocks private ChatRoomService chatRoomService = new
  RedisChatRoomService();
  @Mock private SimpMessagingTemplate webSocketMessagingTemplate;
  @Mock private InstantMessageService instantMessageService;
  @Captor private ArgumentCaptor<String> destinationCaptor;
  @Captor private ArgumentCaptor<InstantMessage> instantMessageCaptor;
  @Captor private ArgumentCaptor<Object> messageObjectCaptor;

  @Test
  public void shouldSendPublicMessage() {
    ChatRoom chatRoom = new ChatRoom("123", "Dream Theater",
    "Discuss about best band ever!");
    ChatRoomUser user = new ChatRoomUser("jorge_acetozi");
    chatRoom.addUser(user);

    assertThat(chatRoom.getNumberOfConnectedUsers(), is(1));

    InstantMessage publicMessage = new InstantMessageBuilder()
        .newMessage()
        .withChatRoomId(chatRoom.getId())
        .publicMessage()
        .fromUser(user.getUsername())
        .withText("This is a public message!");
```

```
chatRoomService.sendPublicMessage(publicMessage);

verify(webSocketMessagingTemplate, times(1))
    .convertAndSend(
        destinationCaptor.capture(),
        messageObjectCaptor.capture());

verify(instantMessageService, times(1))
    .appendInstantMessageToConversations(instantMessageCaptor.
    capture());

String sentDestination = destinationCaptor.getValue();
InstantMessage sentMessage = (InstantMessage)
messageObjectCaptor.getValue();
InstantMessage instantMessageToBeAppendedToConversations =
instantMessageCaptor.getValue();

assertThat(sentDestination, is(Destinations.ChatRoom.
publicMessages(chatRoom.getId())));
assertEquals(publicMessage, sentMessage);
assertEquals(publicMessage,
instantMessageToBeAppendedToConversations);
  }
}
```

The test shouldSendPublicMessage starts creating a new chat room and adds a new user (username *jorge_acetozi*) to it; then it creates a public message that will be sent from jorge_acetozi and invokes the sendPublicMessage method in the chatRoomService method, which is the method you really want to test. After this, it verifies that webSocketMessagingTemplate and instantMessageService were invoked only once and that the destination sent is the "public destination." It also checks that the sent message is the same message that was passed to the sendPublicMessage method before and that the public message is the same that was passed to the appendInstantMessageToConversations method invocation.

CHAPTER 25

Integration Tests

Integration tests are not as straightforward to code as unit tests because they really need to test an entire integration. For example, to test a database integration, you would need to set up this database before running the tests.

To address this issue and avoid the overhead of setting up an entire database just for executing a simple test, many people run integration tests with an in-memory database such as H2.[1]

The point here is that integration tests are more effective when running in an environment similar to the production environment. For example, an in-memory database doesn't have all the features that MySQL has. Some specific MySQL functions will not be able to be tested if you are not running a MySQL instance, right?

So, to make the environment as similar as possible to production, you can use a handy library called testcontainers[2] that allows you to create Docker containers from inside a JUnit test. This is really good because the tests will run against real Cassandra, MySQL, Redis, and RabbitMQ volatile instances.

25.1 Setting Up Dependencies for Starting Docker Containers from JUnit

To use testcontainers, first you need to declare the dependency to pom.xml.

```
<dependency>
  <groupId>org.testcontainers</groupId>
  <artifactId>testcontainers</artifactId>
  <version>1.1.9</version>
</dependency>
```

---

[1] www.h2database.com/
[2] https://www.testcontainers.org/

The following code is executed before running the integration tests. Basically, it sets up Docker containers for Cassandra, MySQL, Redis, and RabbitMQ with STOMP support using the testcontainers library. Note that the waitForMysqlContainerStartup method assures that the integration tests will be executed only after the MySQL container is ready to receive connections.

```java
public class AbstractIntegrationTest {
  @ClassRule
  public static final GenericContainer cassandra = new FixedHostPort
  GenericContainer("cassandra:3.0")
    .withFixedExposedPort(9042, 9042);

  @ClassRule
  public static final GenericContainer mysql = new FixedHostPort
  GenericContainer("mysql:5.7")
    .withFixedExposedPort(3306, 3306)
    .withEnv("MYSQL_DATABASE",  "ebook_chat")
    .withEnv("MYSQL_ROOT_PASSWORD",  "root");

  @ClassRule
  public static final GenericContainer redis = new FixedHostPort
  GenericContainer("redis:3.0.6")
    .withFixedExposedPort(6379, 6379);

  @ClassRule
  public static final GenericContainer rabbitmq = new FixedHostPort
  GenericContainer("jorgeacetozi/rabbitmq-stomp:3.6")
    .withFixedExposedPort(61613,  61613)
    .withExposedPorts(61613);

  @BeforeClass
  public static void waitForMysqlContainerStartup() throws
  InterruptedException, TimeoutException {
    WaitingConsumer consumer = new WaitingConsumer();
    mysql.followOutput(consumer);
    consumer.waitUntil(frame ->
      frame.getUtf8String().contains("mysqld: ready for
      connections."), 90, TimeUnit.SECONDS);
  }
}
```

25.2 JUnit Suites

Setting up Cassandra, MySQL, Redis, and RabbitMQ before every test would require a lot of overhead and be time-consuming. To instantiate these dependencies only once and use them with all integration tests that are executed, you can use a JUnit suite.[3] Basically, a JUnit suite is used to aggregate tests. In the chat application, there are two suites: UnitTestsSuite.java and IntegrationTestsSuite.java. Each one groups all unit and integration tests, respectively.

```
@RunWith(Suite.class)
@Suite.SuiteClasses({
  InstantMessageBuilderTest.class,
  DestinationsTest.class,
  SystemMessagesTest.class,
  RedisChatRoomServiceTest.class
})
public class UnitTestsSuite {

}

@RunWith(Suite.class)
@Suite.SuiteClasses({
  CassandraInstantMessageServiceTest.class,
  RedisChatRoomServiceTest.class,
  DefaultUserServiceTest.class,
  AuthenticationControllerTest.class,
  ChatRoomControllerTest.class
})
public class IntegrationTestsSuite extends AbstractIntegrationTest {

}
```

These two JUnit suites will help you split unit and integration tests so that you can run them on different Maven phases.[4]

---

[3]https://github.com/junit-team/junit4/wiki/aggregating-tests-in-suites
[4]https://maven.apache.org/guides/introduction/introduction-to-the-lifecycle.html

25.3   RedisChatRoomServiceTest.java

The RedisChatRoomServiceTest.java class tests the RedisChatRoomService class, which provides methods for chat room operations.

```java
@RunWith(SpringRunner.class)
@EbookChatTest
public class RedisChatRoomServiceTest {
  @Autowired private ChatRoomService chatRoomService;
  @Autowired private ChatRoomRepository chatRoomRepository;
  @Autowired private InstantMessageRepository instantMessageRepository;

  private ChatRoom chatRoom;

  @Before
  public void setup() {
    chatRoom = new ChatRoom("123", "Dream Theater", "Discuss about
    best band ever!");
    chatRoomService.save(chatRoom);
  }

  @After
  public void destroy() {
    chatRoomRepository.delete(chatRoom);
    instantMessageRepository.deleteAll();
  }

  @Test
  public void shouldJoinUsersToChatRoom() {
    assertThat(chatRoom.getNumberOfConnectedUsers(), is(0));

    ChatRoomUser jorgeAcetozi = new ChatRoomUser("jorge_acetozi");
    ChatRoomUser johnPetrucci = new ChatRoomUser("john_petrucci");

    chatRoomService.join(jorgeAcetozi, chatRoom);
    assertThat(chatRoom.getNumberOfConnectedUsers(), is(1));

    chatRoomService.join(johnPetrucci, chatRoom);
    assertThat(chatRoom.getNumberOfConnectedUsers(), is(2));

    ChatRoom dreamTheaterChatRoom = chatRoomService.
    findById(chatRoom.getId());
```

```
    List<ChatRoomUser> connectedUsers = dreamTheaterChatRoom.
    getConnectedUsers();

    assertThat(connectedUsers.contains(jorgeAcetozi), is(true));
    assertThat(connectedUsers.contains(johnPetrucci), is(true));
  }

@Test
  public void shouldLeaveUsersFromChatRoom() {
    ChatRoomUser jorgeAcetozi = new ChatRoomUser("jorge_acetozi");
    ChatRoomUser johnPetrucci = new ChatRoomUser("john_petrucci");

    chatRoomService.join(jorgeAcetozi, chatRoom);
    chatRoomService.join(johnPetrucci, chatRoom);
    assertThat(chatRoom.getNumberOfConnectedUsers(), is(2));

    chatRoomService.leave(jorgeAcetozi, chatRoom);
    chatRoomService.leave(johnPetrucci, chatRoom);
    assertThat(chatRoom.getNumberOfConnectedUsers(), is(0));
  }
}
```

Basically, shouldJoinUsersToChatRoom creates two users, jorgeAcetozi and johnPetrucci; it joins jorgeAcetozi to the chat room; and it verifies that the chat room now has one connected user. After that, it joins johnPetrucci and verifies that the chat room now has two connected users. Each of these join calls actually hits the Redis instance. Then, it fetches the chat room from Redis and verifies that both jorgeAcetozi and johnPetrucci are connected to it.

The shouldLeaveUsersFromChatRoom class has pretty similar logic.

25.4   ChatRoomControllerTest.java

The ChatRoomControllerTest.java class tests the ChatRoomController class, which provides the REST endpoint for creating a new chat room. Basically, in these two tests, you want to assure that a user without the ROLE_ADMIN role is not able to create a chat room.

```
@RunWith(SpringRunner.class)
@EbookChatTest
@WebAppConfiguration
public class ChatRoomControllerTest {
```

```java
@Autowired
private WebApplicationContext wac;

@Autowired
private FilterChainProxy springSecurityFilter;

private MockMvc mockMvc;

@Before
public void setup() {
  this.mockMvc = MockMvcBuilders
    .webAppContextSetup(this.wac)
    .addFilter(springSecurityFilter)
    .build();
}

@Test
public void shouldCreateChatRoomWhenUserHasRoleAdmin() throws
Exception {
  ChatRoom chatRoom = new ChatRoom("123",
      "Dream Theater",
      "Discuss about best band ever!");

  this.mockMvc.perform(
    post("/chatroom")
          .with(user("admin").roles("ADMIN"))
          .contentType(MediaType.APPLICATION_JSON)
          .content(new ObjectMapper().writeValueAsString(chatRoom))
        )
  .andDo(print())
  .andExpect(status().isCreated())
        .andExpect(jsonPath("$.id",is(chatRoom.getId())))
        .andExpect(jsonPath("$.name",  is(chatRoom.getName())))
        .andExpect(jsonPath("$.description", is(chatRoom.
        getDescription()))));
}

@Test
public void shouldNotCreateChatRoomWhenUserDoesntHaveRoleAdmin()
throws Exception {
```

```
ChatRoom chatRoom = new ChatRoom("123", "Dream Theater",
"Discuss about best band ever!");

this.mockMvc.perform(
        post("/chatroom")
        .with(user("xuxa").roles("USER"))
        .contentType(MediaType.APPLICATION_JSON)
        .content(new ObjectMapper().writeValueAsString(chatRoom))
    )
    .andDo(print())
    .andExpect(status().isForbidden());
  }
}
```

In the shouldCreateChatRoomWhenUserHasRoleAdmin test, the POST request to /chatroom is performed by using an admin user, and it asserts that the response status code is 201 CREATED and that the HTTP response body contains the JSON with the new chat room.

In the shouldNotCreateChatRoomWhenUserDoesntHaveRoleAdmin test, the POST request to /chatroom is performed using a user with ROLE_USER, and it asserts that the response status code is 403 FORBIDDEN.

CHAPTER 26

Splitting Unit Tests from Integration Tests Using Maven Plug-ins

Remember from Chapter 23 that different types of tests have different feedback levels (and hence different performances)? Let's verify this in practice now.

Open a terminal window, go to the ebook-chat directory, and issue the following command:

```
$ mvn test
```

This will execute the class UnitTestsSuite.java, that is, all the unit tests. Note how fast it is to execute these unit tests.

Now issue the following command:

```
$ mvn verify
```

This will execute both UnitTestsSuite.java and IntegrationTestsSuite.java. Note how integration tests take much more time to run.

⚠ This will work only if you followed the steps in Chapter 2. Note that the integration tests will start Docker containers for Cassandra, Redis, MySQL, and RabbitMQ, so none of these containers must be running on your machine when you issue the mvn verify command because that would cause port conflicts.

ℹ You can also run the integration tests by invoking the mvn integration-test command.

It may be a good idea to run the unit tests separate from the integration tests in some cases. To get faster feedback (when something crashes perhaps) while you are writing code, you can run the unit tests as many times as you need without "losing time" waiting for integration tests. (Just don't forget to run both the unit and integration tests at least once before committing the code.)

26.1 Maven Surefire Plug-in

When using Apache Maven to manage the application build life cycle, you can use plug-ins to customize the behavior.

ℹ Apache Maven is extensible, so you could even create your own Maven plug-in[1] if needed.

You can use the Maven Surefire plug-in[2] during the Maven test phase of the build life cycle to execute the unit tests of an application. Here is the plug-in configuration being used in the chat app's pom.xml file:

```
<plugin>
        <groupId>org.apache.maven.plugins</groupId>
        <artifactId>maven-surefire-plugin</artifactId>
        <configuration>
                <includes>
                        <include>**/UnitTestsSuite.java</include>
                </includes>
        </configuration>
</plugin>
```

Note that the configuration is quite simple. It just includes the UnitTestsSuite.java JUnit suite to run all the unit tests when the maven test command is issued. That's it for unit tests!

---

[1]https://maven.apache.org/plugin-developers/index.html
[2]http://maven.apache.org/surefire/maven-surefire-plugin/

26.2   Maven Failsafe Plug-in

The Maven Failsafe plug-in[3] is designed to manage integration tests. Here is its configuration:

```
<plugin>
        <groupId>org.apache.maven.plugins</groupId>
        <artifactId>maven-failsafe-plugin</artifactId>
        <configuration>
                <includes>
                        <include>**/UnitTestsSuite.java</include>
                        <include>**/IntegrationTestsSuite.java
                        </include>
                </includes>
        </configuration>
</plugin>
```

Similarly, it includes the UnitTestsSuite.java and IntegrationTestsSuite.java JUnit suites to run all the unit and integration tests when the mvn integration-test or mvn verify command is issued.

---

[3]http://maven.apache.org/surefire/maven-failsafe-plugin/

CHAPTER 27

Continuous Integration Server

As the chat application grows, running integration tests on a developer's machine becomes a boring task because it starts consuming a lot of time. Can you see the problem that could emerge? The application has good test coverage, but the developer doesn't run the tests because they take too much time (the developer's machine is not a powerful server, right?). Well, having tests and not running them is the same as not having tests, and you already know that having no tests is not a good idea!

It would be reasonable to run all the application tests every time the source code changes in the version control system, wouldn't it? But you already saw that a developer's machine may not be the best place to do this. So, what if you start a dedicated server that automatically does this for you every time a new commit emerges in the version control system? That would be amazing! That's exactly what a continuous integration (CI) server is used for (and more!). There are many tools that allow you to set up a CI server on a machine or a cluster of machines. Probably the most well-known is Jenkins[1] because it has a great community and a huge number of plug-ins.

---

[1]https://jenkins.io/

© Jorge Acetozi 2017
J. Acetozi, *Pro Java Clustering and Scalability*, DOI 10.1007/978-1-4842-2985-9_27

Appendix

Here you will find topics that do not fit perfectly into the main content of this book.

Resource Bundle

The chat application is able to display the text in two languages, English and Portuguese.

messages.properties

This is the default resource bundle that will be used when the user doesn't specify any other locale. It shows the text in English.

```
menu.language=Language
menu.language.english=English
menu.language.portuguese=Portuguese
menu.chatrooms=Chat Rooms
menu.new.chatrooms=New Chat Room
menu.logout=Logout
menu.leave.chatroom=Leave Chat Room

login.title=Login
login.your.username=Your username
login.your.password=Your password
login.username=Username
login.password=Password
login.signin=Sign In
login.create.account=Or create an account
login.badCredentials=Invalid username or password
```

© Jorge Acetozi 2017

J. Acetozi, *Pro Java Clustering and Scalability*, DOI 10.1007/978-1-4842-2985-9

```
new.account.title=New Account
new.account.name=Name
new.account.email=Email
new.account.username=Username
new.account.password=Password
new.account.your.name=Your name
new.account.your.email=Your email
new.account.your.username=Your username
new.account.your.password=Your password
new.account.create=Create
new.account.username.already.exists=Username already exists

chat.available.chatrooms=Available Chat Rooms
chat.chatrooms.name=Name
chat.chatrooms.description=Description
chat.chatrooms.connectedUsers=Connected Users
chat.chatrooms.join=Join
chat.new.chatroom.title=New Chat Room
chat.new.chatroom.name=Name
chat.new.chatroom.description=Description
chat.new.chatroom.close=Close
chat.new.chatroom.create=Create

chatroom.title=Chat Room
chatroom.users=Users
chatroom.public.messages=I want to send public messages
chatroom.message.placeholder=Type your message...
chatroom.send=Send

NotEmpty=May not be empty
Size.user.username=Must have between 5 and 15 characters
Size.user.password=Must have at least 5 characters
Email=Specify a valid email address
```

messages_pt.properties

This is the resource bundle that will be used when the user changes the locale to pt. It shows the text in Portuguese.

```
menu.language=Idioma
menu.language.english=Inglês
menu.language.portuguese=Português
menu.chatrooms=Salas de Bate-Papo
menu.new.chatrooms=Nova Sala de Bate-Papo
```

```
menu.logout=Sair
menu.leave.chatroom=Sair da Sala de Bate-Papo

login.title=Entrar
login.your.username=Seu nome de usuário
login.your.password=sua senha
login.username=Nome de Usuário
login.password=Senha
login.signin=Entrar
login.create.account=Ou crie sua conta
login.badCredentials=Nome de usuário ou senha inválidos

new.account.title=Nova Conta
new.account.name=Nome
new.account.email=Email
new.account.username=Nome de Usuário
new.account.password=Senha
new.account.your.name=Seu nome
new.account.your.email=Seu email
new.account.your.username=Seu nome de usuário
new.account.your.password=Sua senha
new.account.create=Criar
new.account.username.already.exists=Nome de usuário já cadastrado

chat.available.chatrooms=Salas de Bate-Papo Disponíveis
chat.chatrooms.name=Nome
chat.chatrooms.description=Descrição
chat.chatrooms.connectedUsers=Usuários Conectados
chat.chatrooms.join=Entrar
chat.new.chatroom.title=Nova Sala de Bate Papo
chat.new.chatroom.name=Nome
chat.new.chatroom.description=Descrição
chat.new.chatroom.close=Fechar
chat.new.chatroom.create=Criar

chatroom.title=Sala de Bate Papo
chatroom.users=Usuários
chatroom.public.messages=Quero enviar mensagens públicas
chatroom.message.placeholder=Escreva sua mensagem...
chatroom.send=Enviar

NotEmpty=Não deve estar vazio
Size.user.username=Deve ter entre 5 e 15 caracteres
Size.user.password=Deve ter pelo menos 5 caracteres
Email=Especifique um endereço de email válido
```

AFTERWORD

What's Next?

Congratulations, you have reached the end of this book! I hope you have learned a lot and that you now have a good understanding of NoSQL, Cassandra, Redis, Spring, WebSocket, and many other subjects addressed in this book.

The question now is, what's next? I covered a lot of topics in this book, but as you know, the code is running locally on your machine. The next step is to create an entire automated infrastructure so you can implement a continuous delivery pipeline and release the chat application to production in a fast and reliable manner.

To make that happen, there are a number of new concepts involved, such as the following:

- Cloud computing

- Infrastructure as code

- Configuration management

- Security

- Containerization

- Virtualization

In addition, when an application is deployed to a production environment, many things can go wrong, especially if it's available on the Internet, which is not a controlled environment. To be notified about and react quickly to issues that may happen in production, relying on a set of real-time monitoring tools is crucial.

If you are interested in learning about these subjects in depth, I invite you to take a look at the online courses, e-books, and articles available on my web site.[1]

Thank you very much for reading this book.

—Jorge Acetozi

---

[1] https://www.jorgeacetozi.com

J. Acetozi, *Pro Java Clustering and Scalability*, DOI 10.1007/978-1-4842-2985-9

Index

© Jorge Acetozi 2017
J. Acetozi, *Pro Java Clustering and Scalability*, DOI 10.1007/978-1-4842-2985-9

Get the eBook for only $5!

Why limit yourself?

With most of our titles available in both PDF and ePUB format, you can access your content wherever and however you wish—on your PC, phone, tablet, or reader.

Since you've purchased this print book, we are happy to offer you the eBook for just $5.

To learn more, go to http://www.apress.com/companion or contact support@apress.com.

Apress®